Fearless Female
SOLDIERS, EXPLORERS, AND AVIATORS

Bessie
Coleman

FIRST FEMALE AFRICAN AMERICAN
AND NATIVE AMERICAN PILOT

CATHLEEN SMALL

Cavendish
Square
New York

Dedication: To my dad, Steven Snyder, who introduced me to my love of flight. I hope in the afterlife, you've finally gotten to climb into the cockpit of your beloved P-51 Mustang.

Published in 2018 by Cavendish Square Publishing, LLC
243 5th Avenue, Suite 136, New York, NY 10016

Copyright © 2018 by Cavendish Square Publishing, LLC

First Edition

Website: cavendishsq.com

This publication represents the opinions and views of the author based on his or her personal experience, knowledge, and research. The information in this book serves as a general guide only. The author and publisher have used their best efforts in preparing this book and disclaim liability rising directly or indirectly from the use and application of this book.

CPSIA Compliance Information: Batch #CS17CSQ

All websites were available and accurate when this book was sent to press.

Library of Congress Cataloging-in-Publication Data

Names: Small, Cathleen, author.
Title: Bessie Coleman : first female African American and Native American pilot / Cathleen Small.
Description: New York : Cavendish Square Publishing, [2018] |
Series: Fearless female soldiers, explorers, and aviators |
Includes bibliographical references and index.
Identifiers: LCCN 2016058598 (print) | LCCN 2016059782 (ebook)
ISBN 9781502627537 (library bound) | ISBN 9781502627544 (E-book)
Subjects: LCSH: Coleman, Bessie, 1896-1926–Juvenile literature. |
Air pilots–United States–Biography–Juvenile literature. |
African American women air pilots–Biography–Juvenile literature. |
Indian women air pilots–Biography–Juvenile literature.
Classification: LCC TL540.C646 S63 2018 (print) | LCC TL540.C646 (ebook) |
DDC 629.13092 [B] —dc23
LC record available at https://lccn.loc.gov/2016058598

Editorial Director: David McNamara
Editor: Stacy Orlando
Copy Editor: Nathan Heidelberger
Associate Art Director: Amy Greenan
Designer: Stephanie Flecha
Production Coordinator: Karol Szymczuk
Photo Research: J8 Media

Printed in the United States of America

Contents

one

The Times of Bessie Coleman

"The air is the only place free from prejudices." —Bessie Coleman

Bessie Coleman's life was relatively short by modern standards, but the thirty-four years in which she lived—1892 to 1926—were remarkable. Not only were there new developments in aviation and technology, but the social landscape in America was also changing. Post–Civil War political battles and debates around gender and racial civil rights were still going on, and tensions continued through World War I and beyond. It is nothing short of amazing that Coleman succeeded in this era to become a female pilot, and even more incredible is that she was both African American and Native American. In a time when segregation was

Oppostite: Fearless young aviatrix Bessie Coleman earned her international pilot's license in 1921.

commonplace, minorities were seen as less than whites, and women did not even have the right to vote, Bessie Coleman managed to persevere and break past those stereotypes and gain fame as the first female African American and Native American pilot.

A South Without Slavery

Less than three decades before Bessie Coleman was born, the Civil War ended, and the **Emancipation Proclamation** was enforced, ending slavery in the South (the North had abolished slavery much earlier, by 1804). In Texas, where Coleman's family lived, slaves were officially granted their freedom on June 19, 1865, a day now remembered as **Juneteenth.** The next few years were known as the **Reconstruction Era**, and the military ensured that slaves in the South were indeed freed and not enslaved again.

This was a major change in society—and one that many Southerners had difficulty accepting. Even those who didn't resent the abolishment of slavery still had to adjust to a new dynamic in which African Americans were free and looking for work to support their families.

Any change like this is bound to be slow moving and met with resistance, and this is certainly the case with the end of slavery. When troops began to leave the South after Reconstruction, African Americans again found themselves at the mercy of white people—only this time, in positions of **involuntary servitude**. Bessie Coleman's parents found themselves in this type of servitude as "sharecroppers." Sharecroppers were allowed to farm the land, but only if a portion of their crops went to the landowner.

The sharecropping arrangements were appealing at first for newly freed black and poor white families because they could not afford to purchase their own land, but many found themselves in exploitative arrangements with no prospect of improving the situation. In other words, African Americans, though no longer slaves, were still controlled and restricted in every aspect of their lives.

Racial Tensions in the South

In 1890, Mississippi passed laws to officially **disenfranchise** both blacks and whites living in poverty. Nine more former Confederate states followed suit in the next two decades. These laws instituted poll taxes, residency requirements, record-keeping requirements, and literacy and comprehension tests that effectively stripped African Americans and poor whites of their right to vote. Racial discrimination in the South permeated all aspects of life.

The disenfranchisement laws created an unbalanced political system and stripped African Americans of any political rights. Since African Americans couldn't vote, the elections unsurprisingly went to the candidates supported by wealthy Caucasians—and often those candidates had no interest in improving conditions for blacks. Without any sort of political voice, African American communities suffered. For example, public facilities, such as libraries and schools, were underfunded. A vicious cycle was created. African Americans could not pass the literacy requirements or afford the poll taxes required to vote, and so their community had no political voice, which meant that their facilities suffered. Thus the children using those facilities got substandard educations and ended up living in the same cycle of poverty as their parents had.

As women, Bessie Coleman and her mother were at a dual disadvantage. They could not vote because they were women, and they also would have difficulty voting because they faced the same challenges as other African Americans. Women were not granted the right to vote until the Nineteenth Amendment was ratified in 1920.

Segregated areas, as in this 1940s picture of a bus station waiting room in North Carolina, were the norm in the Jim Crow South.

This problem went beyond local politics, too. In 1912, Southern-born (but Northern-dwelling) Woodrow Wilson was elected president of the United States, and he appointed Southern politicians to **cabinet** positions. Wilson and his cabinet members quickly decided that racial separation would create the best possible nation for white people and African Americans, and they supported segregated workplaces along with legislation that upheld segregation.

In Texas, where Bessie Coleman was born and raised, segregation was vividly apparent. The railroad tracks in Waxahachie, where she grew up, geographically divided the white and black neighborhoods. **Jim Crow laws** dictated where African Americans could drink water from, where they could eat, which restrooms they could use, and more. Segregated railroad cars were instituted in 1891, and further laws were enacted in the years that followed. In 1910, segregated waiting rooms were added to the laws about railroads, and around that same time segregated water fountains and restrooms were introduced into legislation.

All across the South, racial tensions were high, and all too often they resulted in conflict and death. In 1892, forty African Americans were jailed in Memphis, Tennessee, following incidents at a cooperative known as the Peoples Grocery, which was owned and managed by eleven black men. During one altercation, shop owners attempted to protect their store from an attack by a group of armed white men. After the arrests, a white mob subsequently pulled Tommie Moss, Will Stewart, and Calvin McDowell from their jail cells, took them outside of the city, and murdered the three men.

Closer to Coleman's home, in Paris, Texas, a crowd tortured an African American teenager, Henry Smith, who was accused of raping a young girl in 1893. Smith was the subject of a nationwide manhunt. Following his capture, railroads brought in spectators, and schoolchildren were allowed to leave their classes to go watch the killing. Smith was branded with hot irons and burned. His death was a public spectacle.

Lynchings were common. Female African American journalist Ida B. Wells found that 728 African Americans had been lynched in the South over a ten-year period, equating to six deaths per month. In New York City and New Orleans there were two major riots in 1900, during which many African Americans were lynched. In the New York City riot, ten thousand young white people—some civilians and some police officers—attacked any and all African Americans they encountered over a four-day stretch. By some miracle, only one man died, but many more were injured. The New Orleans riot, which also included a few other areas in the Deep South, resulted in the deaths of at least twenty-eight African Americans as a response to a black man who had shot a white police officer.

Race riots again occurred September 22–24, 1906, in Atlanta, Georgia, sparked by Democratic candidates for governor who were threatened by the impact of the black vote on the election. M. Hoke Smith and Clark Howell both had ties to news publications, and they used the media to launch a scare campaign and circulate unsubstantiated stories of black men attacking white women. The candidates were trying to appeal to white voters by promising to control African Americans, whose success in the Atlanta area was somehow threatening to the white population. In response, a white mob raided black businesses and homes. At least twenty-five African Americans and two European Americans were killed during the violence over those two days.

It did not help that the entire country was in the midst of an economic depression, leading to high unemployment. In Texas, where cotton was king, an infestation of boll weevils had left many cotton farmers in dire circumstances. Bessie Coleman grew up amid widespread poverty and unemployment, as well as racial turmoil. It is thought that between 1880 and 1950, a total of thirty-five thousand African Americans were tortured and murdered by white mobs, often in front of spectators.

Great Migration to the Segregated North

Although the South was a hotbed of racial tension, discrimination did not exist *only* in the South. Northern cities and states experienced tension, too—the New York City race riots were one example, but there were riots in Springfield, Illinois, and other cities as well. Indeed, segregation also existed heavily even in the North. Chicago was known as a city where African Americans could prosper, but it was strongly racially divided, with black people occupying specific neighborhoods in the South Side.

Bessie Coleman briefly left Texas to attend college in Oklahoma, but she returned home after one term, when her money for school ran out. She was restless, though. Texas was the same old place of limited opportunities and discrimination, and she wanted more from life. Even though Chicago and the North had their own issues with racial tension and segregation, it seemed a better place to try to make a life than Texas. So, in 1915, at the age of twenty-three, Coleman bid farewell to Texas and made her way to Chicago, where two of her brothers were waiting.

Promise of a Better Life

Coleman was not alone in relocating to Chicago. The year 1915 marks the start of the Great Migration, in which six million African Americans left the South and moved to the North

The South Side of Chicago in the early 1900s had many African American neighborhoods.

and West. This movement continued until 1970. Black people were fleeing racial tensions, Jim Crow laws, segregation, and injustice in the South, but they were also lured to the North and West by the promise of jobs and a better future. Northern companies actually sent recruiting scouts to the South to try to entice laborers to relocate and work in their factories.

Chicago was a prime destination for those relocating during the Great Migration. The African American population in the city in 1890 was very small, less than 2 percent, but by the time World War I occurred (1914–1918), the African American population in the city had doubled to roughly 4 percent, or about one hundred thousand residents. It continued to grow as African Americans flocked to the city. Part of that was due to Chicago-area companies recruiting labor from the South, but an even bigger factor was the African American newspaper the *Chicago Defender*, which actively encouraged people to "leave that benighted land [the South]."

Motivation from the Press

The *Chicago Defender* was perhaps the nation's most influential black weekly newspaper of the time. It was smuggled south and circulated among black communities because white distributers refused to sell the paper and copies were often confiscated by groups such as the Ku Klux Klan. Nevertheless, the paper was extremely popular and played a significant role in the Great Migration. The *Defender* took a particular interest in the northern movement of African Americans, often publishing stories on the front page. According to the paper, one city that promised a better life was Chicago. The paper claimed, "To die from the bite of the frost is far more glorious than that of the mob," and pointed out that African Americans could earn up to eight dollars a day working for the railroads in Chicago.

Indeed, there was the potential for prosperity for African Americans in Chicago. Illinois was quite progressive with its antidiscrimination laws. School and public accommodation segregation had been outlawed in 1874 and 1885, respectively. The schools were better for children, which families hoped would break the cycle of uneducated poverty they had been living in for so long. There was work for African Americans in Chicago—often as railroad porters, as Coleman's brother Walter was. It was respectable employment for an African American man in Chicago, though certainly not an easy job. The work was exhausting, and the white clients were demanding. African Americans who worked overnight were degraded and forced to sleep on worn blue sheets in order to prove that they were not soiling the same white sheets that the white passengers slept on. It was not a perfect situation, but to many it was better than sharecropping.

Being a woman, Coleman faced additional challenges. There might have been work for African American men in Chicago, but opportunities for women were more limited. Just as in the South, she could do domestic work as a maid, cook, or laundress. She could also pursue cosmetology and become a hairstylist or a manicurist. Coleman ultimately chose the latter option.

Better but Still Separate

The ethnic divide of Chicago was not entirely unlike the town in Texas where Coleman grew up, which had the white and black neighborhoods physically separated by railroad tracks. Even before African Americans began migrating to Chicago, it was a very ethnically divided city. There were many immigrants from various parts of Europe, and they tended to inhabit specific neighborhoods. For example, the Irish immigrants in the city inhabited the South Side—at least, they did until the African Americans began moving in.

The South Side of Chicago was home to steel and meatpacking industries and thus had many working-class jobs that appealed to the incoming African Americans. They learned about the predominantly black neighborhoods from the *Chicago Defender* and from friends who had preceded them. As they arrived, they began to populate the South Side heavily, particularly in eight or nine well-known African American neighborhoods. The area became known as the **Black Belt** and stretched for about thirty blocks along State Street. Its north and south borders were at Twelfth Street and Thirty-Ninth Street, respectively, and its east and west borders were Lake Michigan and Wentworth Avenue, respectively.

The Black Belt slowly expanded as African Americans moved into predominantly white areas. If a house in the neighborhood sold to an African American family, it would often provoke a mass exodus of white people who sold their homes and moved out of the city.

Local realtors who took advantage of this trend were known as "blockbusters." They would sell one house in a neighborhood to an African American, and using the fear that more minorities would move in the neighborhood, they would convince white families to react by putting their houses up for sale at low prices. The agents then sold the properties at higher prices, earning double profits. In this way, white families began to push out into the suburbs—Chicago had (and still does have) an extensive public transportation system, so men could easily commute

Flight Begins

Although racial tensions dominated the South around the turn of the century, violence did not always impact day-to-day life. In many ways, life still progressed as normal—particularly for white Americans. People went to work and raised their families, and they kept pursuing interests as normal.

This was a very good thing for Bessie Coleman because without the work of two white men in North Carolina, she might never have made history. Brothers Orville and Wilbur Wright, both from Dayton, Ohio, were hard at work trying to unravel the mysteries of flight. They had honed their mechanical skills by working in their machine shop with such devices as printing presses, bicycles, and motors, but their true interest was in flight. Aviation enthusiasts had long studied birds and machinery, wondering how to connect the two. How could machinery help humans achieve flight in the same way that birds do? Some felt more powerful engines were the answer, whereas others felt that movable wings, like birds have, were the key. The Wright brothers eventually discovered the real answer: a three-axis control that would allow the pilot to steer and balance the airplane. Using data they gathered from extensive wind-tunnel experiments and their own attempts at building a craft that could fly, they developed the device that made fixed-wing flight possible.

The brothers were certain that maintaining equilibrium in the aircraft was essential. Winds could change and gust at any time, and they believed that the pilot would need complete

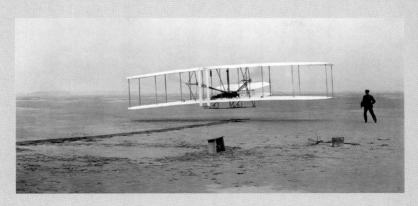

The Wright Brothers piloted their *Wright Flyer* in 1903.

control over the aircraft to be able to compensate for the changing air. With this in mind, they set the goal to master gliding before attempting flight in a motor-drive aircraft. They spent a couple of years working on gliding, which they finally felt they had comfortably conquered in late 1902. Finally, they were ready to move on to powered aircraft, and they built the *Wright Flyer I* out of giant spruce wood in 1903.

To test their powered plane, they needed a location with generally mild breezes and preferably a relatively soft landing surface, so they selected Kitty Hawk, North Carolina. It was there, on December 17, 1903, when Bessie Coleman was not yet twelve years old, that the first successful controlled, sustained flight of a heavier-than-air human aircraft occurred. From there, aviation technology took off (literally and figuratively!) and rapidly developed into what Bessie Coleman experienced when she first slid behind the controls in the cockpit in late 1920.

into the city to work but move their families out of the diverse areas of the city. This made room for minorities—including African Americans—to move into neighborhoods in the city, such as those in the Black Belt.

When Coleman moved to Chicago, the Black Belt was still a relatively nice place to live. Just as in the white neighborhoods, the African American neighborhoods had rich areas and poor areas. The two lived together in relative harmony for a while—there was not a lot of tension between the richer African American families and the poorer ones. The culture and arts of the area were strong, too. In jazz clubs and other nighttime hot spots, talented musicians such as Louis Armstrong and Bessie Smith performed, and blacks and whites often danced and mingled in the same spaces, despite the segregation in many other aspects of life. Coleman worked in an area known as "The Stroll," which stretched along State Street for eight blocks, between Thirty-First and Thirty-Ninth Streets. Bessie Coleman biographer Doris L. Rich cites historians who called the area a "black Wall Street and Broadway." It was a place to be seen and a place to be. It was also the place to get liquor if you wanted it. Prohibition went into effect in 1920, but booze was readily available at the clubs on The Stroll.

However, as more and more African Americans and other immigrants moved to Chicago, the living situation began to deteriorate. The city wasn't built to accommodate such a strong influx of people, and the lower-income areas became overcrowded. The city couldn't support appropriate sanitation services for the growing population, for example, so regular garbage collection didn't always happen. The city also couldn't keep up with building inspections, which sometimes led to dangerous living situations. The city police put a low emphasis on crime prevention and control in the South Side neighborhoods, which obviously led to higher crime rates. Over the years, much of the Black Belt became a slum, but when Bessie Coleman moved there in 1915, it was still a land of the promise of a brighter future.

Racial Tensions in the North

This is not to say the Black Belt was untouched by racial tensions. In fact, the Chicago race riot of 1919 spanned nearly a week and was particularly bloody. Thirty-eight people died (twenty-three of them African American), more than five hundred suffered injuries, and one thousand African American families had their homes burned down. Although Coleman's family was unharmed, in her own neighborhood a ten-year-old African American boy, Joe Crawford, had to flee his family's home and seek shelter when a white neighbor warned Joe's mother that a group of white teenagers planned to publicly flog her and Joe. In her book *Queen Bess: Devil Aviator*, Rich states the teens reportedly mobbed the Crawfords' building and yelled, "Come out and get your asses whipped or stay in there and be barbecued!" Given the brutalities that had been inflicted on African Americans across the nation for many years, it's not surprising that Joe and his mother took the angry mob at their word.

The Chicago race riot of 1919 was part of a string of riots that occurred across the nation in the summer and fall of 1919, and Chicago's was considered among the worst of them. Certainly, it was the worst race riot Illinois had seen, with six thousand members of the National Guard called in to stem the riot.

The Rise and Fall of Texas Cotton

Before oil became a dominant industry in Texas, there was cotton. Spanish missionaries in the region grew the crop in the 1700s, and by the mid-1800s, Texas was in the top ten cotton-producing states in North America. Production temporarily decreased during the Civil War, but after the war was over, the cotton business picked up again.

In the post–Civil War era, many people migrated to Texas to work the cotton fields, including many African Americans from the Deep South. Most worked as sharecroppers or tenants on large farms owned by white landowners. The tenants would live on the property and supply their own seed, tools, and draft animals, and they would work the land under the hot Texas sun, from planting in the spring, to summer cultivation, to picking and ginning starting in late summer. For their hard work, tenants typically got to keep two-thirds of the value of the cotton they sold. They had to turn over one-third of their profits to the landowner. Sharecroppers, like Bessie Coleman's family, only got to keep half of the cotton profit because in their case they supplied only labor—the landowner supplied the seed, tools, draft animals, and living quarters. The take-home profit was barely enough to cover living expenses, and definitely not enough for things like savings and higher education.

The cotton industry in Texas suffered an enormous blow when the insidious boll weevil made its way north from Mexico in the late nineteenth century. The tiny, devastating beetle

Cotton was the primary industry in the South, and many African Americans worked in the fields.

marched north and destroyed crops in Texas and the rest of the Cotton Belt that ranged throughout the Deep South. Cotton farmers got a temporary reprieve when World War I came around because it brought with it an increased demand for cotton. Yet once the war ended, cotton prices dropped, and many tenants and sharecroppers left farming in pursuit of a better, more sustainable income.

The riot of 1919 was set off on July 27, 1919, when a seventeen-year-old African American boy, Eugene Williams, floated on a homemade raft into the white area of Lake Michigan. Chicago was a largely desegregated city, although the neighborhoods were certainly distinct. There were no laws enforcing "Whites Only" areas or public facilities. Yet Lake

During the 1919 race riot in Chicago, the National Guard was called in to restore order.

Michigan's beaches were unofficially segregated, with black areas and white areas. When Eugene Williams inadvertently floated into the white area, he was stoned to death by a group of young white men. The white man who incited the stoning was identified by an eyewitness, but Chicago police refused to arrest him and instead arrested an African American man. African American observers protested and were swiftly attacked by whites, at which point it became an all-out battle between the white and black communities.

The racial explosion had been a long time coming. While military members from Chicago had been off fighting in World War I, the people moving into the area had filled their jobs in factories and warehouses. Servicemen returned home in late 1918 and early 1919 to find that they no longer had jobs or a way to support themselves or their families. On the other side, black veterans were frustrated because they had fought in the war alongside whites and were still treated as second-class citizens upon their return home to Chicago.

Meanwhile, the unofficial segregation of neighborhoods in Chicago had become more official when the Chicago Real Estate Board began stepping in and setting up **homeowners' associations** (HOAs) that enforced segregation and dictated where and how African Americans and other minorities could live. So-called **New Negroes** eschewed peaceful acquiescence to segregation and Jim Crow laws and promoted armed self-defense of the African American neighborhoods.

At this point, Chicago was largely controlled by white Protestant men. In 1915, filmmaker D. W. Griffith released a three-hour silent film called *The Birth of a Nation*, which was a commercial success and widely seen by Americans. The film not-so-subtly portrayed the Ku Klux Klan as heroic white

Protestants and the only logical ruling force in the nation, while simultaneously depicting African Americans as aggressive and unintelligent. It was a white supremacist's dream, a bit of a love letter to the Ku Klux Klan. The **NAACP** tried to get the

The popular film *The Birth of a Nation* was protested by members of the NAACP, as seen here at a theater in Flushing, New York.

racist film banned, but they failed in their efforts. In fact, the film ended up being the first American movie screened at the White House—under President Woodrow Wilson, who firmly believed in segregation.

It's easy to see how the film and the segregation of Chicago—even if largely unofficial—contributed to perceptions of African Americans as "others" who were not truly equal to the whites in the city. Despite Chicago and the North not being as overtly racist as the South, the unspoken tensions certainly contributed to division between the races, even in a progressive city. By 1930, fifteen years after Coleman moved to the city, the negative perception about African Americans still existed. As Rich asserts in *Queen Bess*, one Chicago historian of the day described the typical African American as "a virtual savage from the cotton fields … [He might] don clothes and something of the manner of the urban dweller, [but] the Negro, half-child, half-man, was still the under dog [sic]. He was still a 'separate' being … He was delighted when white people treated him nicely."

two

A Texas Childhood

"Susan Coleman wanted her daughter to grow up experiencing lots of opportunities. But she knew Bessie would have an uphill struggle."
—Connie Plantz

Bessie Coleman grew up in rural Texas in the late 1800s, the daughter of sharecroppers. The days were long and the work backbreaking, but Coleman's childhood filled her with a desire to achieve more than what she saw her peers doing in Texas.

Opposite: Bessie Coleman was commemorated by the United States Postal Service with this 1995 stamp.

Atlanta, Texas, circa 1904. Farmers wait to unload their potato crops.

Welcome to Atlanta

The name Atlanta brings to mind the capital of Georgia, and also its most heavily populated city. However, Atlanta, Texas, a tiny city named for the much larger city in Georgia, is a world apart from that booming metropolis. While Atlanta, Georgia, boasts a population of roughly half a million people, Atlanta, Texas, has about 5,600 residents. Back in the late 1800s, when Bessie Coleman was born there, Atlanta, Texas, had a population of just over 1,700 people.

Atlanta was a fairly new town when Coleman was born on January 26, 1892. It had been established just two decades before, in 1871, and it quickly grew to 1,500 residents by around 1885. The growth slowed, and by the time Coleman was born, the town's population had leveled out and was starting to decline.

Although Atlanta's main industry was lumber, that wasn't what had drawn Coleman's parents there. They were sharecroppers working the cotton fields. George Coleman was part African American and part Native American; one of his grandparents was African American, and the other three were of the Cherokee or Choctaw tribes. George's wife, Susan, was African American and was likely born into slavery. No definitive records exist about whether she was a slave, but she was born in Georgia, which was a slaveholding state, so it is believed that she was. Being three-quarters Native American and only one-quarter African American, it is likely that George was born free.

Atlanta had a fairly substantial African American community, so the family fit in well in this small town located on the far east side of Texas, less than 10 miles (16 kilometers) from the Arkansas and Louisiana borders.

The Coleman Family

Coleman was the tenth of George and Susan's thirteen children, born when her mother was thirty-seven years old. Her birth date is believed to be January 26, 1892, though no birth certificate exists and her parents did not record her birth in a family Bible (a common practice at the time). When Coleman was born, there were six children plus George and Susan living in a one-room cabin with a dirt floor on a dirt road. Four of George and Susan's thirteen children did not survive past infancy, which was not uncommon for African American families in those days.

In the late nineteenth and early twentieth centuries, mortality rates for African Americans of all ages were substantially higher than those for whites living in similar areas—that is, when comparing blacks living in rural southern areas to whites living in similar areas, the mortality rates were significantly higher for African Americans. No definitive answer for this disparity has been found, but it is thought to be linked to a number of causes, including less access to good medical care, a high number of tuberculosis cases, poor nutrition, and other factors faced by African Americans. So while today we would see four infant deaths in one family as shocking, for an African American family in the late 1800s, it wasn't unusual.

In that little one-room cabin, Coleman was particularly close to her older brother John, who looked after her while their mother and father were busy with work and family chores. John would read Bible passages to Coleman while she sat in his lap at night, and throughout the day he kept her clean and safe from harm.

When Coleman was two years old, her family underwent a transition. A new baby girl, Elois, was born, and the family relocated west to Waxahachie, Texas, outside of Dallas.

Waxahachie is now known as the Gingerbread City, but it wasn't as idyllic as the name might imply when Coleman grew up there.

Moving Up to Waxahachie

Waxahachie isn't exactly a large town, either. When Bessie Coleman's family moved there in 1894, the population was less than four thousand people. Still, compared to tiny Atlanta, it was quite a change.

George Coleman spent his entire life savings—about twenty-five dollars—on a 0.25-acre (0.1-hectare) parcel on Mustang Creek, fronting Palmer Road, in Waxahachie. With the move came larger living quarters, surrounded by a willow tree and fruit trees. George built a rectangular "shotgun house," a major improvement from the family's old one-room house on a dirt road. The new house had three rooms lined up front to back in such a way that it was said if you fired a shot through the front of the house, it could pass straight through all the rooms and exit out the back. Narrow shotgun houses were particularly popular in the Southern United States in the late 1800s and early 1900s, and many can still be found in New Orleans, where the style was quite popular. They were common in lower- and middle-class African American neighborhoods like the one where George moved his family in October 1894.

The house was small, but certainly bigger than where they had come from. Susan made it cheerful and homey by planting yellow and red roses, lilacs, honeysuckle vines, and a garden with sweet corn and peanuts.

The Cotton Industry

The Colemans were one of many African American families to move to Waxahachie during that time. The city was located in Ellis County, the largest producer of cotton in the United States. All around the city were cotton yards, cotton warehouses, and cotton mills, which meant lots of jobs for eager workers. Ellis County's cotton production boomed in the fifty-year period from 1860 to 1910, going from 389 bales of cotton produced annually to 106,384 produced annually.

It was ambition that led George to move the family to Waxahachie, in search of the relative fortune that came with "white gold," as some cotton farmers referred to their crops. The Colemans quickly settled into their new neighborhood east of the railroad tracks, where the African American community lived. During that time, segregation was still very much in force; blacks didn't live in white neighborhoods and vice versa. Jim Crow laws ensured that African Americans had designated places to eat, drink, sleep, sit, and go to school, and that those areas did not reach into white areas. "Whites Only" signs designated all of the spaces where African Americans weren't welcome, including bathrooms, restaurants, movie theaters, and even drinking fountains.

As segregated as that lifestyle sounds, it was all the Colemans had ever known. After all, slavery had officially only just ended thirty years before, and many blacks, particularly in the South, were still getting used to the idea of being free to live their own lives. The fact that their personal lives were wholly apart from those of whites was just a way of life back then, and it would be a long time before that sort of separation ended.

Daily Life

The Coleman family made their home in the African American part of town, establishing friendships and becoming part of the Baptist Church in Waxahachie. Susan Coleman was devoutly religious and insisted that the family spend all of Sunday at church. Susan gave birth to her last two children: daughters Nilus in 1896 and Georgia in 1898. In 1898, Bessie Coleman started school. However, it was often interrupted when she had to care for her younger siblings while her mother worked.

By 1900, eight-year-old Bessie Coleman was the oldest daughter left at home. Her older sisters Lillah and Alberta, ages twenty-five and twenty-one, respectively, had left home, as had brother Walter, seventeen. Isaiah and John, ages fifteen and eleven respectively, were still at home, but boys were not expected to do much to care for younger siblings if there was a female around to do the work.

On days she attended school, Coleman would walk 4 miles (6.4 km) to a one-room school for black children. It was a good school, but not overly remarkable. The teachers worked hard to establish a feeling of black pride and instill a sense of confidence in the students, but otherwise it was a fairly standard school. At that time, teachers at African American schools didn't require any licensing, and many had only a sixth-grade education themselves. Susan Coleman was thrilled to watch young Bessie learn to read and write, skills that she herself did not have. She wanted her children to find more opportunities than she had, and education was the first step to doing so.

As it turned out, Bessie Coleman was drawn to reading and would spend hours doing it once she learned. The library wagon came by their house a couple of times a year, and Susan would pick up books for Coleman, such as biographies of strong African Americans, including Booker T. Washington and Harriet Tubman, and poems by African American poets. Coleman was particularly affected by Harriet Beecher Stowe's account of slavery in the South, chronicled in *Uncle Tom's Cabin*, and she vowed never to let her life be dictated by the cruelty of slavery.

A New Head of the Household

In those days, the man was generally the head of the household; 85 percent of black households had a man at the head of the family. Yet George Coleman relinquished that right when he decided to leave the family. He was resentful of the stratified social situation in Waxahachie and the Jim Crow laws that dictated how his family could live and where they were allowed to go. He was also disgusted by the fact that he wasn't allowed to vote because he couldn't read, write, or pay the poll taxes. Additionally, he was a bit of a walking target in Texas: not only was he African American, which made him a likely candidate for lynching if he dared challenge the status quo or step out of line in any way, but he was also Native American, which in Texas was even more despised than being African American.

George decided to move to Oklahoma, which at that point was considered "Indian Territory," a region set aside by the US government for Native Americans. As part Choctaw, George and his family could live in an area where they would be treated as equals. As biographer Connie Plantz states in *The Life of Bessie Coleman*, Susan refused to move, saying, "I am neither a pioneer or squaw." It should be noted that the term "squaw" is now viewed as offensive to many modern Native Americans because it has been used to demean

African American women, including Coleman's mother, often worked as domestics, but Bessie knew that job wasn't for her.

Native women; however, it is possible Susan used it simply to say she was not Native American.

To Susan, it wasn't a great loss. Although her husband had been ambitious in moving from Atlanta to Waxahachie, in general she found him to be rather lazy. So, without fanfare or complaint, Susan took on the position as head of the household, giving Bessie Coleman and her siblings a strong female role model to look up to.

Susan took a job as a cook and housekeeper for a white couple named Mr. and Mrs. Elwin Jones, who lived on the other side of town. They were a kind couple, but the wages were still very low. Coleman's two older brothers, Isaiah and John, left and went north. Isaiah moved to Canada to farm in the Amber Valley outside of Edmonton, and John, to whom Coleman had been so close when she was very young, moved to Chicago to live with another one of their siblings, Walter.

The Coleman family remaining in Waxahachie had to get creative to make ends meet. Susan often brought home food from the couple she worked for, including biscuits and cooked steak, among other things. She also brought home hand-me-down clothes for the girls, some of them hardly worn at all by the Jones girls. This practice of white employers giving black employees food or other gifts was very common at the time. It was called "pan toting" or "service pan," and it was a way that white employers attempted to justify the very low wages they paid. A higher wage would have of course been preferable, but like the segregated social situation at that time, it was just the way it was.

Susan made the best of her job situation. She studied her employers' living practices and manners and taught them to her children. Her daughters learned etiquette customary in white society by sitting at a table covered in a tablecloth, learning to use the correct forks and spoons for different meal courses, and practicing the expected manners. Although Susan wanted her children to be proud of their African American identity, she also wanted them to have opportunities which she had not, and she knew that knowledge of how to behave in white society could only benefit them.

Working from a Young Age

Since Susan's job didn't pay enough to support a large family, the children who were old enough went to work in the field to help out, and Bessie Coleman was among them. She and her sisters would miss school to help plant, pick, and chop cotton in the fields. This was a common practice among sharecropping families. The school ran an adjusted schedule and was not in session from August to December, to accommodate for children who helped during the harvest. However, many children still were unable to attend at other times of the year, when the school was open.

Working the cotton fields was backbreaking labor. Despite being under ten years old, Coleman was expected to guide a mule-driven plow through the hot fields, drop the seeds into the plowed soil, and then pack the tilled earth around them. As the cotton bushes grew, Coleman had to trim, thin, and weed the scratchy plants, wearing a long-sleeved dress even in the hot sun to protect her arms. At harvest time, she worked alongside her siblings, picking cotton balls and stuffing them in bags. A good laborer would pick between 150 and 200 pounds (68 to

91 kilograms) of cotton a day—surely more than Coleman's entire body weight!

Not surprisingly, cotton farming was not Coleman's favorite activity; she would have rather been reading. Farming was expected of her, so she did it, while dreaming of a life that would hold something more. Ultimately, she found she had strength in math and record keeping, which was a great help to her family. Each day, the family members had to weigh the cotton they had picked, and Coleman would record it on paper, along with the price per pound. If the foreman was not looking when her family weighed their cotton, Coleman would slyly put a foot on the scale to increase the weight. She could also figure out how much money her family should be paid by the white man who owned and oversaw their land.

Striving for More

Coleman was ambitious, even then. Her bookkeeping abilities kept her family from being cheated out of what they were owed for the cotton they harvested, and she developed strong sales skills by selling tickets for their church bazaar, which ultimately won her a harmonica for selling more tickets than anyone else. She was devoted to her religion as well, and became a minister of the Missionary Baptist Church when she was twelve years old.

The one-room schoolhouse only went up to eighth grade, and Coleman finished all eight grades. She wanted to go on to college to expand her opportunities, but there was no extra money for that to happen. It was all Susan could do to make ends meet for the family at home. So, Bessie

Who Is Jim Crow?

The Jim Crow laws in the Southern United States were not named after an actual individual person. In fact, "Jim Crow" was a derogatory name people used to refer to African Americans. It originally came from the popularity of white actor Thomas D. Rice's 1830s song-and-dance caricatures of blacks known as "Jump Jim Crow." In 1892, the *New York Times* published an article about voting laws in the South that referred to "Jim Crow laws."

What exactly were Jim Crow laws? Simply put, they were laws to ensure that racial segregation stayed intact. The laws governed where African Americans could attend school, eat, drink, and use the restroom, and they governed how African Americans could do things like use public transportation. These laws existed at the state and local levels, and they were generally enacted after the Reconstruction Era, which lasted until approximately 1877, and continued through the 1960s.

Jim Crow laws were particularly prominent in the South; discrimination existed in the North, but it was subtler. The South blatantly disenfranchised blacks and passed laws enforcing segregation. African Americans may have had schools, restaurants, churches, and nearly everything else that white people had, but the facilities were underfunded and generally inferior. The neighborhoods were poor; the government may have claimed blacks had separate but equal status to whites, but in reality they did not.

Jim Crow laws existed in the United States until the 1960s, but even after the civil rights movement and changes in the law to make segregation illegal, truly eradicating the Jim Crow mentality took much, much longer. Certain segments of the population would still like to return to the Jim Crow South of the early twentieth century, but most US citizens now recognize how truly divided and unequal that time was.

Segregated drinking fountains were a common sight in the South.

Coleman took a job doing laundry and began stockpiling her earnings to put toward college.

It was an incredibly ambitious goal. In the early 1900s, not very many Americans attended college, and only about 3 percent of Americans graduated from a university. Roughly 60 percent of those graduates were men as not many women attended college. The numbers were even lower for women of color, like Coleman. Just as college today is expensive, so was college back then. In 1900, an education at a relatively prestigious university ran about $150 per year. It doesn't sound like much now, but Coleman's job as a laundress earned her a mere $4 to $8 per month. To put it in perspective, Coleman had to work for nearly two years just to earn enough money to pay for a year of college education.

It was hard work, too. Every Monday, Coleman went across town to the white area and collected dirty laundry from the families. Because African Americans were not welcome at the front door of white homes, she would knock on the back door to collect the laundry, and then she would trudge back across town to her own small shotgun-style house to begin the process of washing and ironing clothes. She had to get water from the well and boil it in a pot, adding the clothes to the boiling pot. Then, she had to use homemade lye soap, a very caustic soap, to hand-scrub the clothes on a washboard. Coleman would rinse and starch the clothes, wring them out by hand, and then hang them to dry. Finally, she would use an iron heated on the stove to press out all the wrinkles. Then, every Saturday, she would walk back across town to deliver the clean, ironed clothing to her customers.

Her pay was subject to the mercy of the white families, too. If she lost a sock or the family wasn't happy with the clean laundry for some other reason, she simply did not get paid, and she had no recourse but to accept it.

Still, Coleman persevered, and at age eighteen, in 1910, she entered the Colored Agricultural and Normal University in rural Langston, Oklahoma (now known as Langston University).

College Days

At the university, Bessie Coleman became Elizabeth Coleman, which she felt was more elegant than the name her parents had given her and had given to census takers after she was born. She had to begin in the school's preparatory section, which was designed for students who didn't meet the school's entrance requirements. Because Coleman's one-room school in Waxahachie had only gone up to eighth grade, and because she had missed much school while working in the cotton fields, she did not meet the university requirements. She instead found herself in the sixth-grade level of the preparatory school.

Unfortunately, Coleman's days as a laundress had only yielded enough money for one school term, so she had to return to Waxahachie after completing just one term at the Colored Agricultural and Normal University. Yet she did so with the style befitting a showman: she convinced the Langston band to come home with her so that she could step off the train onto the platform a hero, with her own band to play at a homecoming party. Even at a young age, Coleman knew a bit about showmanship.

Lincoln Beachey:
The Father of Acrobatics

One of the best-known pilots of Bessie Coleman's time was Lincoln Beachey, a young man from San Francisco who started out by flying **dirigibles**. By 1910, he was flying both balloons and fixed-wing aircraft at air shows, and in 1911 he had a chance to fulfill a dream: he got to fill in for an injured pilot at a Los Angeles air show.

As it turned out, Beachey gained even more fame from that air show than he could have expected. His plane's motor failed at 3,000 feet (914 meters) and went into a nose-diving spin. At that time, no pilot had ever survived a spin like that. However, Beachey turned his plane into the spin and regained control of his aircraft, cementing himself as a master of flight.

Beachey liked to prove that he could do the impossible, as he did when regaining control of his doomed plane. Later in 1911, he decided to try to win $1,000 by being the first person to fly a plane over Niagara Falls. In the midst of his flight, he changed plans. After circling over the falls multiple times, he piloted his plane down into the mist and flew it under a bridge and back up the other side, stunning the 150,000 spectators. The crowd at the 1911 Chicago International Aviation Meet was similarly wowed when he raced a train and let the plane's wheels touch the top of the moving train as it passed underneath him.

Beachey is credited with inventing numerous acrobatic flight techniques, including vertical drops, figure eights, and

LINCOLN BEACHEY, THE WORLD'S MOST DARING AVIATOR.

Lincoln Beachey, the Father of Acrobatics, was also known as "The Man Who Owns the Sky."

loops. He also set a world altitude record of more than 11,000 feet (3,353 m) when he filled up his plane's fuel tanks and vowed to climb upward until he ran out of gas. He did just that, and when the engine finally sputtered and died at 11,578 feet (3,529 m), he glided it in slow spirals to the ground, landing safely once again.

Beachey's career was short but glorious. In 1915, on his first public flight in a **monoplane** he'd had built, Beachey was flying the plane upside down when he realized his altitude was too low. He tried to pull the plane up, but the strain of doing so caused part of the wings to break, and his plane plummeted into San Francisco Bay. Still, in his five years as a master acrobatic pilot, Lincoln Beachey achieved more than enough to inspire young aviators like Bessie Coleman to want to try the same.

Coleman's desire to learn and do something more with her life didn't end with the end of her college days. Her mind continued to spin with possibilities.

Back in Waxahachie

When Coleman returned to Waxahachie, she also returned to working as a laundress. While doing the mindless but strenuous work, she thought about her future and what the possibilities might be. One thing that fascinated her was flying. The Wright brothers had made their historic first flight less than a decade before, in December 1903, and in the years since, the field of aviation had made tremendous gains.

Looking to the Skies

Despite the gains in technology, aviation was a mysterious and frightening endeavor to many. Newspapers covered the many accidents that occurred in the early days of flight, blaming the high speeds at which the planes flew—60 miles per hour (96.5 kilometers per hour) was scandalously fast in those days—and mysterious holes in the sky (a theory later proven to be false).

In the United States and Europe, men were increasingly interested in this new technology and were taking to the skies. In 1910, France's Raymonde de Laroche became the first licensed female pilot in the world. This was more than a decade before Amelia Earhart began to fly, and female pilots, or aviatrixes, were a rare occurrence. Even more rare were African American pilots. In fact, until 1912, they didn't even exist. In March of that year, Emory C. Malick became the first licensed African American pilot in the United States. For a long time, it was

Elise Raymonde Deroche adopted the stage name Raymonde de Laroche when she was an actress. The French aviatrix later became the first woman in the world to receive a pilot's license.

believed that James H. Banning, who received his pilot's license in 1926, was the first African American aviator. But in 2004, one of Malick's great-nieces found evidence proving that Malick was, in fact, the first African American pilot in the United States.

The fact that Bessie Coleman, an African American woman, was able to enter a field so heavily dominated by white male pilots is nothing short of amazing. She ultimately had to go to France to earn her license, and eventually she achieved her goal. Perhaps, during her time back home, flying was simply a passing fantasy of doing something more than living out her life as a laundress or a sharecropper, but eventually she would dedicate herself to making that dream come true.

three

Moving North and Taking to the Skies

"Between 1915 and 1970, six million African Americans left their homes in the South and moved to states in the North and West."
—Hana Layson with Kenneth Warren

Bessie Coleman may not have had much formal education, but she was intelligent and forward thinking. She knew she wanted more out of her life than being a laundress in Waxahachie, Texas. Thus, in 1915, at the age of twenty-three, she headed north for the promise of an exciting new life.

Opposite: Coleman often had a big smile in her pictures, but she had a serious side, too.

Moving North

Back in the early 1900s, a trip to Chicago wasn't as easy as it is today, and especially not if you were African American. The journey from Texas to Chicago required a twenty-hour train ride for which travelers typically dressed in their "Sunday best" clothes, normally only worn for special occasions or to church on Sunday.

If you were black, you had two choices of where to ride on the train: you could travel in the all-black car or in the Jim Crow section of the men's smoking car. Neither of these options was particularly pleasant. In the smoking car, stale smoke hung heavy in the air, and in the all-black car there was just one single toilet that quickly became filthy with so many people using it. The seating was simply a hard wooden bench, which didn't make for the most comfortable twenty-hour journey. Coleman clutched suitcases with all of her belongings and a sack of food for that long, twenty-hour journey.

It would be worth her trouble, she hoped. Coleman's older brother, Walter, said she could stay in his apartment when she arrived. To Coleman, pretty much anything was better than life scrubbing other people's laundry in rural Texas. At the end of the journey, she arrived safely in Chicago and made her way to Walter's apartment in the Black Belt of the South Side.

Walter had moved to Chicago more than a decade before, and now, at age thirty-five, he was working as a Pullman porter for none other than the son of Abraham Lincoln. While Abraham Lincoln may have abolished slavery, blacks were not yet seen as equal to whites, and Robert Todd Lincoln's businesses model enforced separation. He ensured that blacks were segregated from whites in almost every way. Walter and his fellow porters had to sleep on sheets designated for African Americans, drink from separate water fountains, and use separate restrooms.

Along with Walter, Coleman lived with Walter's wife, Willie, who she found very bossy and not particularly likeable. Coleman tolerated her, though, because she wanted to stay in Chicago and didn't have any other place to live. They also lived with Coleman's brother John, who had tended to her when she was a young child, and his wife, Elizabeth. Neither couple had children, so it was an apartment full of adults.

Working in Chicago

While Walter worked hard at his job with the Pullman Company and assumed the role as the provider of the house, John was frequently unemployed and tended to drink too much. Bessie Coleman, like Walter, was a hard worker, so she immediately looked for work when she arrived. Most jobs open to women at that time were either as domestics (cooks, laundresses, or maids) or as schoolteachers. Coleman didn't care to do either of those because she could have easily done those same jobs in Texas. Wanting something more, she settled on becoming a beautician.

This was actually a surprisingly controversial move. Although the South Side was full of beauty shops, some people felt that beauticians basically helped black women to look more white by bleaching their skin and straightening their hair. Critics such as educator Nannie Helen Burroughs were disgusted with this practice, saying, "What every woman who bleaches and straightens out needs is not her appearance changed, but her mind changed … If Negro women would use half the time they spend on trying to get white, to get better, the race would move forward apace."

BEST YET!
FOR ALL THE FAMILY!

MADAM WALKER'S
ALL-PURPOSE
HAIR CONDITIONING
CREAM

"FOR PERFECT DRESSING AND GROOMING"

Before she became an aviatrix, Coleman worked in the
beauty field. Many products were marketed to African
American women to condition or straighten their hair.

Coleman was not discouraged. She enjoyed experimenting
with fashion, makeup, and hairstyles, and she didn't see it as
in any way denouncing her African American heritage. She
saw it as a job that she enjoyed and could make a living at.
With that in mind, she enrolled in a manicuring course at the
Burnham School of Beauty Culture.

In fact, Coleman turned out to be both a talented
manicurist and a shrewd one. In 1916, she won a contest for
the best and fastest manicurist in Chicago. She decided to
stick with manicuring partly because she was good at it and
partly because she could start working right away, whereas
learning to be a hairdresser would take more courses and
much more time.

Coleman quickly found a job as a manicurist for men
at a shop on the Stroll section of State Street. She was quite

successful because she was good at doing manicures. She was also pretty and charming, and it so happened that men liked to have their nails done by her. Many of her customers admired her and left large tips in appreciation.

Making Connections

When Coleman wasn't working, she explored the area. The Stroll was full of restaurants, bars, nightclubs, and shops, and Coleman knew them all: the Elite Club #2, Royal Garden, Pekin Café, and Dreamland. These were hotspots for African American performers such as Louis Armstrong and Bessie Smith. They were also good places to get liquor, particularly after Prohibition went into effect, and Coleman's brother John knew them well. In his spotty employment history, he had worked as a cook for bootleggers and gangsters, and those same powerful men came to Bessie Coleman for manicures.

Living in Chicago, Coleman fairly quickly grew to know a large network of people, some of them quite prominent. One such person was Robert Abbott, the founder, editor, and publisher of the *Chicago Defender*, the most widely circulated black-owned newspaper of the time. Abbott used to stand at the corner of Thirty-Fifth and State Streets, elegantly dressed and with a cigar in his mouth, and talk to community leaders.

Coleman was intrigued and eventually began to mingle with Abbott and other important men in the area, such as Jesse Binga. Binga had been a Pullman porter and a barber, but he abandoned both pursuits in favor of real estate. He not only renovated and rented properties, but through the practice of blockbusting he also made a significant amount of money. Binga ultimately opened his own private bank for African Americans.

Robert Abbott (*right*) was the head of the very popular
Chicago Defender.

It has been rumored, but never confirmed, that Coleman had an affair with Binga. Not surprisingly, this was not something Coleman would openly admit to. Binga was incredibly unpopular with many people; he was powerful but hated. According to Doris L. Rich, one former employee said of Binga, "He was a mean son-of-a-bitch." In fact, he was so unpopular that his house was bombed seven times in two years.

Coleman was no stranger to men of questionable ethics. One of the other friends she made during this time was Oscar De Priest, Chicago's only African American alderman, later turned United States congressman. De Priest was tried for corruption in 1917, but he was ultimately acquitted. Coleman was also friendly with Anthony Overton, founder of a bank that failed when it became known that Overton had invested all of the bank's capital in one of his own businesses.

A Mysterious Choice

Despite being friendly with all of these powerful (albeit ethically questionable) men, Coleman did not show any interest in forming a long-term romantic relationship with any of them. In fact, she didn't show any interest in marrying anyone, although she likely could have had her pick of bachelors. In those days, many women aspired to get married, but not Coleman. She was more intent on making something of herself than on securing a man.

It is therefore intriguing that she suddenly married Claude Glenn, a friend of her brother Walter. Glenn was fourteen years older than Coleman when they married shortly after her twenty-fifth birthday. The marriage is a mystery because it is not clear whether any of Coleman's family knew about it. Certainly it existed; a marriage license was issued to the pair on December 30, 1916, and the marriage was recorded at the bottom of the certificate when it occurred. It was reportedly performed by Baptist minister John F. Thomas at an apartment near Walter's. Shortly after the marriage, Coleman moved out of Walter's apartment into her own on Forest Avenue; however, there is no record at all that Claude Glenn ever lived there with her. Nor is there any record of Coleman living at another address with Claude Glenn.

Coleman's sister Elois made no mention of the marriage in her memoirs. Additionally, it appears Coleman's four nieces and nephews did not recall her being married either. Two of the nieces even lived with Coleman for a time, and while they remember "Uncle Claude," a pleasant, quiet man, visiting Coleman, they assumed he was a family friend, and Coleman never told them otherwise.

By all accounts, no one who knew her is sure why Coleman would have married Claude. He was a pleasant man, certainly, but Coleman didn't show any sign of being attracted to him. His personality wasn't the dynamic type that Coleman seemed usually drawn to. He wasn't poor, but he certainly wasn't wealthy. He got by, just as Coleman and her brother did. It appears that perhaps Coleman considered him a good friend and perhaps married him solely for that reason. Conceivably, Coleman just was not the marrying type, and thus an unconventional marriage suited her just fine. American marriages in the 1900s tended to place women in a subservient role, which was something Coleman certainly didn't appreciate.

The Coleman family women did not particularly cling to the notion, also held in the 1900s, that a woman had to get married and stay married. Susan, Bessie Coleman's mother, had parted ways with Coleman's father, considering him lazy and not particularly worth staying married to. Likewise, Coleman's youngest sister, Georgia, left behind the father of her baby daughter Marion and moved to Chicago in 1917. It's unknown whether Georgia and he had even been married. Marion once asked about her father when she was older, and Georgia simply replied, "I couldn't stand him."

Additionally, Coleman's younger sister Elois moved to Chicago in 1918 with her four children, Eulah B., Vera, Julius, and Dean. They left behind Elois's husband, Lyle Burnett Stallworth, who was abusive and beat Elois. By this point, Susan had also moved to Chicago (with Georgia and Marion), and finally Nilus, Coleman's other younger sister, joined them with her four-year-old son, Arthur. She, too, left her husband behind, for reasons unknown. Clearly, the Coleman women were not ones to stay in a bad marriage just for the sake of following the conventional path.

Coleman lived comfortably and happily in Chicago, with her family around her. She enjoyed her job, but still, she wanted to do something more. Her inspiration to do so came from a somewhat unlikely place—her ne'er-do-well brother, John.

Committing to a Dream

One fall day in 1919, Coleman's brother John, back from World War I, stopped by the barbershop where Coleman was working her manicure station. He was not entirely sober, and he began teasing Coleman about how French women, whom he had seen while he was stationed in France with the Eighth Army National Guard, were superior to African American women.

John teased Coleman about how the French women could fly, saying, "You [black] women ain't never goin' to fly! Not like those women I saw in France."

The barbershop patrons laughed at John's teasing, but Coleman simply smiled and said, "That's it! You just called it for me!" It seems it was in that moment that Coleman's passion was strengthened. She had been interested in flight before, but it was not until John threw down the challenge that Coleman committed to making it a reality: she would fly, despite her gender and the color of her skin.

Roadblocks to the Sky

There were a few obstacles for her to overcome first. One big problem with Coleman's new goal was that no one wanted to teach her to fly. There were no known African American pilots at that time, so Coleman approached as many white pilots and schools as she could think of. All of them turned her down.

Another barrier she had to face was discrimination against her ethnicity and her gender. She was African American and Native American at a time when none were flying publicly. She was also a woman, and there were very few women in the United States who flew. Furthermore, she was not particularly educated. She certainly did not have a background in anything related to aviation. Although she was extremely confident, this may have been off-putting to the white men in the field.

Having exhausted all her options for flight instruction in America, Coleman went back to the South Side and talked to Robert Abbott. Not only was he the publisher of perhaps the most prominent newspaper of the Great Migration, but as it turned out, he was also the perfect person for Coleman to turn to. He came from a long line of strong, independent women, and thus he believed that women were perfectly capable of accomplishing the same things men could. He also published a paper designed to show that black people were worthy of respect and could accomplish the same things as white people. He believed in Coleman, and she was the perfect subject for his newspaper. If she achieved her goal of learning how to fly, it would make excellent news. So, he was in full support of her goal.

Like Coleman's brother John, Abbott felt France was the place to be for a woman who wanted to achieve this goal. The French were not known for being as racist as Americans, and they led the world in aviation technology. Abbott offered to give Coleman a reference for an aviation school in France if she saved money to go and learned French.

That was all Coleman needed to hear. She enrolled at a language school on Michigan Avenue, and she left her job as a manicurist in favor of a better-paying job as manager of a chili parlor. She saved every penny she could from her new job. Still, it's highly unlikely that she saved enough to pay all of the expenses related to her study in France: ship passage both ways, room, board, and tuition.

There is no evidence of how Coleman obtained enough money to go, but it's thought that Jesse Binga gave her some of it. Positively, he was wealthy enough to do so, and perhaps there was something to the rumors that Coleman was his mistress. Robert Abbott also gave her some of the money she needed. In a May 1926 interview with the *Pittsburgh Courier*, Coleman made mention of a Spaniard who, she said, "made it possible for me to continue my studies in aviation." Her niece Marion suggests that Coleman had a lot of gentleman callers, some of whom spoke other languages, and it's possible the mysterious

The Nieuport 80, a predecessor to the plane Coleman learned to fly in France

Spaniard was one of those. The nature of their relationship—and indeed her relationship with Binga—will never be known, nor will exactly where all of the money came from.

A Small Falsehood

Whatever means she obtained the money by, Coleman had enough money by November 1920 to apply for her passport and contact an accredited aviation school in France. She also told a lie that she would adhere to for the rest of her life: she listed her birthdate as January 20, 1896. Her brother John swore as her character witness that the information was indeed correct, although it was actually four years after her real birthdate.

It's unknown why Coleman chose to lie, but it was likely to avoid any stigma about her age. Although twenty-eight is not old by today's standards, it may have been beneficial in those days to appear younger if you were a woman trying to achieve a goal.

This was actually the first of many public fibs Coleman would tell. Although she was known for being honest with family and friends, Coleman quickly realized that to achieve fame, she needed to have a good story. Up to this point, her story wasn't overly exciting, so she embellished. The press, without the fact-checking practices and tools available today, simply took her at her word and printed what she claimed as the truth.

Less than three weeks after applying, Coleman obtained her passport as well as travel visas for England and France. In 1920, she boarded the SS *Imparator* in New York City, sailing for France.

Bonjour la France!

Finding an aviation school in France didn't turn out to be quite as easy as Coleman might have liked. "I first went to Paris and decided on a school," she said in an October 1921 interview with the *Chicago Defender*. "But the first to which I applied would not take women because two women had lost their lives at the game."

Coleman ended up enrolling at the famous École d'Aviation des Frères Caudron at Le Crotoy in the Somme region in northern France. Le Crotoy is a township in the region that is most famous as being where Joan of Arc was imprisoned before her trial in Rouen. To Bessie Coleman, it was the place where she got to learn how to fly. In seven months, she learned everything from tailspins to banking to loops.

It was an exciting time, but a stressful one. Although Abbott had claimed the French were not racists and allowed people of color to attend flight school, Coleman was one of only three non-Caucasians in her training class, and she was the only one who was black. It was physically demanding as well. Despite it being winter in chilly northern France, Coleman had to walk 9 miles (14.5 km) from her rented room to the airfield every day. She also had signed an accident waiver releasing the school from any responsibility if she were to be injured or killed during training. While training, Coleman saw another student pilot get killed in a flight accident. Coleman said witnessing the accident was a terrible shock but that it did not cause her to lose her nerve, nor her resolve to fly.

Learning to Fly

Coleman trained in a Nieuport Type 82, a common training plane for French pilots. It was a French-manufactured biplane that measured 27 feet (8.2 m) long and had a wingspan of 40 feet (12.2 m). The planes were incredibly fragile, made of wood, wire, steel, aluminum, cloth, and pressed cardboard. The cloth that covered the wings was notorious for peeling off in the air. Although it seems almost unimaginable, this early plane had no steering wheel and no brakes. It was controlled by a baseball bat-sized vertical stick and a foot-controlled rudder bar. The stick was used to control the **pitch** and roll of the plane, while the rudder bar controlled the **yaw**.

Being a novice, Coleman didn't know about steering right away. She sat in the rear cockpit while the instructor sat in the front. Each cockpit had duplicate controls. The instructor in the front cockpit would explain what he was doing as he flew, but Coleman couldn't hear him over the plane's engine and the roar of the wind, so she simply watched what her controls did as the pilot in the front cockpit maneuvered the plane. In studying the movements of the controls and the plane together, she was able to determine how to handle the stick and rudder bar to pilot the plane. To stop the plane, the pilot had to lower the plane's tail so that a rigid metal tail skid would dig into the earth and drag the plane to a stop.

It was a messy, smelly business, too. The pilot would climb in the cockpit, then wait as the mechanic primed the engine with castor oil and started the eighty-horsepower engine. The heat baked her face, and the fine yellow mist from the castor oil coated her goggles and face.

One thing Coleman learned was that she liked to fly at high altitudes. Her reasoning, as she told the *Chicago Defender* in October 1921, was that "the higher you fly, the better the chance you have [to correct for the error] in case of an accident."

Madame Aviatrix

In June of 1921, after seven months of training, Coleman took her licensing test from the Fédération Aéronautique Internationale (FAI), the only organization that offered international licenses at that time. To pass, she flew a 3.1-mile

(5 km) closed-circuit course twice, climbed to an altitude of 164 feet (50 m), performed a figure eight, landed within 164 feet (50 m) of a designated point, and turned off the engine before touching down.

Coleman passed easily, and she received her license on June 15, 1921, making her the first internationally licensed African American (and Native American) female pilot. Not only was she the first African American woman to earn a license from the FAI, but she was the only woman of the sixty-two pilots who trained and earned a license with her.

Before heading home to the United States, Coleman spent two months in Paris, supposedly training with a French pilot who had shot down thirty-one planes during World War I. There are no records of her stay, so it's possible that Coleman embellished this part of her story, as she was prone to do. Regardless, it is known that on September 16, 1921, Coleman boarded the SS *Manchuria* in Cherbourg, France, and headed home to New York.

Media Darling

Coleman's return to New York was triumphant. Both black and white reporters met with her in New York to interview the first black aviatrix. Coleman, always a showman and knowing full well that the press would help her gain fame, was more than happy to give interviews.

Along with those interviews came more embellishment. She told the *New York Tribune*, for example, that she had ordered a Nieuport plane to be built for her in France. There is no record that this claim was true. Coleman was not alone in telling exaggerations and lies; most of her fellow aviators

After her much-publicized flight over the ex-kaiser's palace,
Coleman gained much media attention.

embellished similarly. The public worshipped heroes with
glamorous stories, so many aviators spiced up the rather
mundane realities of flying with some exciting details that
more often than not weren't entirely true. Coleman had to
make herself stand out to get coverage in white newspapers.
She was the darling of the *Chicago Defender* and other black
newspapers, but getting featured in a white newspaper was
another story. Her tales had to be good, or she would not
remain worthwhile news for the general public.

Coleman was principled in her tales. She might embellish her stories to get more media attention, but she refused to pass herself off as anything other than a black woman. The *Chicago Herald* offered to run a feature story on her if she agreed to pass as white. Coleman was fairly light-skinned and probably could have pulled it off, but that wasn't her style. Instead, as biographer Doris Rich recounts in *Queen Bess*, Coleman brought her mother and niece, both of whom were dark skinned, to the interview and said with a laugh, "This is my mother and this is my niece. And you want me to pass?"

Amid interviews, Coleman also found time to be the guest of honor at a performance of the musical *Shuffle Along*, an all-black Broadway musical that was a surprising smash hit among white and black audiences. The cast presented Coleman with an engraved silver cup to honor her, and the entire multiethnic audience gave her a standing ovation.

Yet being a celebrity wasn't enough to get a job. At that time, most pilots worked as **barnstormers**, performing on farms where they would charge admission to people who wanted to watch them do aerial acrobatics and would sometimes make extra money by taking people up in their planes. The barnstormers would often sleep in the farmer's barn while using his farmland for the several-day run of the show.

Coleman was a good pilot, but the skills she had gained in France were not enough to make her stand out from the rest of the barnstormers. She decided she ought to go back to France and continue her aviation studies. Just months after arriving in the United States, Coleman returned to New York City and booked a passage back to France on the SS *Paris*.

Coleman had a week before the ship left, so she spent the time with a female friend in Harlem. During her time in Harlem, Coleman became acquainted with George W. Harris, editor of the black weekly newspaper the *New York News*. Harris was alderman of New York City's Twenty-First District, and he accompanied Coleman to what would be her first public speaking engagement, at the Metropolitan Baptist Church. Coleman spoke to the congregation of 2,500 of her time spent in France getting flying lessons, and she told them she was headed back to France to take possession of the Nieuport plane she had supposedly ordered. She also claimed she would be purchasing other planes for her aviation school.

This was a common thread in Coleman's speeches and interviews. After she learned to fly, she was dedicated to the idea of teaching other African Americans to fly. Coleman told the *Chicago Defender* in October 1921, "We must have aviators if we are to keep up with the times. I shall never be satisfied until we have men of the Race who can fly … Of course, it takes one with courage, nerve and ambition. But I am thrilled to know we have men who are physically fit; now what is needed is men who are not afraid of death." Coleman frequently spoke of the aviation school and her desire for men and women of color to fly. She spent years and much effort trying to pull together the needed money to start her aviation school. Unfortunately, that part of her dream never came to fruition; she died before ever starting the school.

Alderman Harris ultimately became Coleman's manager. He was second in a line of many, though. Whether the men were unfit for the job or whether Coleman's strong personality turned them off, she went through several managers over the course of her career.

Return to Europe

In an effort to improve her skills, Coleman returned to France in late February 1922. She spent two months taking advanced flight lessons in a Nieuport plane (the one she supposedly bought never did make an appearance). After leaving Paris, Coleman moved on to Holland, where she met with Anton H. G. Fokker, who had designed planes for the German air force during World War I.

Fokker invited Coleman to tour his plant and fly some of his planes, and Coleman later told an American reporter that she had persuaded Fokker to come to America to build planes and set up an inclusive aviation school that would offer lessons to men and women regardless of race or religion. Fokker did indeed move to the United States shortly thereafter to build and sell planes, but there's no record of him ever setting up an aviation school. Either it was a dream that never materialized or it was another embellishment on Coleman's part.

After meeting with Fokker, Coleman moved on to Germany, where she spent ten weeks. Pathé News, a British producer of newsreels and documentaries, filmed Coleman in Berlin, flying a plane over the defeated **kaiser's** palace. Coleman got hold of a copy of the newsreel and showed it at the lectures she gave in the United States when she returned.

Back to the United States Again

Bessie Coleman finally returned to the United States on August 13, 1922. Once again, she was met by reporters wanting to do a story on the beautiful young black pilot. By this time she was thirty years old, but she continued to give her age as twenty-four. There was no written record of her birth, and the press and the public accepted the claim that she was indeed twenty-four.

Coleman's interviews tended to contain a mixture of fact and fiction. Some lies were small white lies, but others were outright untruths. For example, she claimed to have learned to fly while working with a Red Cross unit in France. Coleman did indeed learn to fly in France, but she was never part of the Red Cross. Often, her falsehoods centered on the claim that planes had been ordered for her or for her aviation school. Coleman at times was unable to book a show because no one wished to loan her a plane, so she frequently stated that she was awaiting delivery of her own plane in an attempt convince others to let her fly.

Her Big Debut

Upon her return to the United States, Coleman's first public performance was scheduled for August 27, 1922, at Glenn Curtiss Field in Long Island. However, the show was rained out and postponed until the next week, when Coleman already had a show scheduled in Chicago. Although Coleman longed to perform in Chicago, where most of her family was located, she convinced the *Chicago Defender*, which was sponsoring the show, to delay it so she could do the New York show. Thus, on Labor Day in 1922, Bessie Coleman became the first African American and Native American woman to perform a public flight in the United States, in front of a crowd of a few thousand people.

Coleman was not allowed to do any acrobatics because she was flying a borrowed Curtiss JN-4 plane, and the owner had forbidden her to do stunts. Though a sedate flight, the event was still a success. Crowd members were taken up in planes after the exhibition flights, and perhaps thanks to Coleman's appearance, many of those crowd members were African American. J. A. Jackson, an African American columnist covering the event for *Billboard,* wrote on September 15, 1922, that the sightseeing flights for crowd members "did a big business all afternoon. Probably more people of color went up that day than had ever flown since planes were invented." Coleman had achieved her goal of getting people of color in the air; now she just needed to get them into the cockpit.

Further Engagements

Coleman's strong performance in Long Island led to more exhibition flights. Her second show was in Memphis, Tennessee, in front of a crowd of thousands. In September 1922, Coleman, the daredevil aviatrix and queen of the South Side, finally returned home, triumphantly, to Chicago to perform an air show.

On October 2, 1922, the *Chicago Defender* publicized the show with flowery (albeit highly embellished) descriptions of what her performance would entail: "Her flight will be patterned after American, French, Spanish and German methods. The French Nungesser start will be made. The climb will be after the Spanish form of [Bert Acosta] and the turn that of McMullen in the American Curtiss. She will straighten out in the manner of Eddie Rickenbacker and execute glides after the style of the German Richtofen. Landings of the Ralph C. Diggins type will be made."

The *Defender's* publicity was essentially name-dropping in the grandest form. The pilots mentioned were all World War I flying aces—with the "German Richtofen" being a reference to Germany's famed "Red Baron." Interestingly, all of the descriptions of Coleman's flying referred to well-known male pilots, but given the lack of female pilots at that time, it's not entirely surprising.

The *Defender* also mentioned that Coleman's sister Georgia would parachute off the plane in a "drop of death" that no one had ever attempted before. The problem was, no one had cleared this with Georgia. In her memoirs, Elois Patterson, Coleman and Georgia's sister, remembers that Georgia, upon hearing of this, announced, "I will not, absolutely not, jump!" In response, Coleman shouted, "You'll do what I tell you!" and Georgia countered, "Who in the hell do you think you're talking to?" Like Coleman, Georgia was not one to back down, and in this instance, Georgia won the battle. Coleman gave in and arranged for Jack Cope, a veteran wing walker, balloonist, and rope-ladder expert, to do the stunt instead.

The Chicago performance was a success. David L. Behncke, a white businessman and aviation enthusiast, loaned Coleman a plane. Unlike others, he had no issue with her gender or ethnicity, and he trusted her skill as a pilot. Coleman flew Behncke's plane in front of a crowd of two thousand spectators. For Coleman, the most important people in the crowd were her mother, Susan; her sisters, Georgia, Elois, and Nilus; three of her nieces; and her nephew, eight-year-old Arthur Freeman, who was so inspired by his aunt that he later became a pilot.

Making Enemies

Bessie Coleman was no doubt a media darling, but she put her celebrity status in jeopardy when she signed a contract to do an eight-reel feature film tentatively called *Shadow and*

Sunshine, produced by the African American Seminole Film Producing Company. *Billboard* writer J. A. Jackson, who had previously written rave reviews about Coleman's air shows, had connected Coleman with the production team and publicized her appearance in the film. Three weeks later, Coleman abruptly backed out of the film, angering Jackson and many others.

Her reasoning? The filmmakers wanted her to appear in the film's first scene as an ignorant young African American girl, just arriving in New York in worn clothing and with a pack on her back. In other words, they wanted her to play up the part of a poor, ignorant black woman. Coleman, remembering her childhood disgust with some of the hapless characters in *Uncle Tom's Cabin*, flatly refused. She would not support a negative portrayal of an African American person. In November 1922, Jackson reported that as Coleman left the project, she told the production team, "No Uncle Tom stuff for me!"

The film production team and the media portrayed Coleman as a spoiled actress for her decision to abruptly leave the film. The president of the Seminole Company, Peter Jones, told J. A. Jackson that the film's production delay was "because of the temperament of that young lady, who, after coming to New York at the expense of the company, changed her mind and abruptly left New York without notice to the director."

Earning a Bad Reputation

Jackson and Jones weren't the only people Coleman had alienated. Jackson had partnered with Dr. J. H. Love, manager of the Colored State Fair of Raleigh, to form the National Association of Colored Fairs. Their association was aimed at coordinating and booking talent for black state fairs, which were gaining in popularity. Coleman agreed to perform at fairs in Norfolk, Virginia, and Raleigh, North Carolina, in the fall of 1922, but she didn't show up for either engagement.

Not only was she gaining a reputation for being unreliable, but also she had gone through three managers in five months. In an article published on December 1, 1922, Jackson publicly accused Coleman of seeming "to want to capitalize her publicity without being willing to work."

The Aspiration of a School

Clearly, show business was not going to be in Coleman's immediate future. She had alienated too many powerful men affiliated with the industry. So, she headed back to Chicago to pursue her dream of opening a flight school where African Americans could learn to fly. There were two problems: she needed money, and she needed planes.

David Behncke was willing to let her borrow a plane for lessons here and there, but she needed her own planes if she were to actually start an aviation school. While she pondered ways to raise the capital to buy her own planes, Coleman took on the occasional student using Behncke's plane.

One of these students was Robert Paul Sachs, an African American advertising manager for the Coast Tire and Rubber Company of Oakland. Coleman took advantage of the opportunity to propose a plan to Sachs: she would go to California and drop paper advertisements from a plane to promote Coast Tires. She planned to use the money she earned to buy a plane on the West Coast.

California Dreams

Upon arriving in Oakland, Coleman toured the Coast Tire and Rubber Company, and then she gave an interview about the tour and about her agreement to distribute advertising for them from her plane. The interviewer printed the story and also mentioned that Coleman would be opening an aviation school in Oakland. It's unknown if this part of the plan was actually true, or whether it was yet another embellishment on either Coleman's part or the part of the reporter. Coleman did distribute the advertising, but as mentioned, she never did succeed in opening a school.

California was sort of a paradise for aviators. The climate, particularly in Southern California, was ideal for flying—it was sunny and mild, with gentle breezes. If Coleman could fly in the harsh weather of the Midwest, then she could undoubtedly fly there.

After her tour in Oakland, Coleman headed south for the Los Angeles area, where she planned to buy a surplus military plane from the Rockwell Army Intermediate Depot at Coronado. For $400, she was able to buy an early Curtiss JN-4. Naturally, when Coleman was interviewed by the *Air Service News Letter*, she embellished the story. Rather than buying one plane, she claimed she had bought three and was arranging to have them flown to San Francisco as soon as they were built.

Coleman did several interviews at this time. In addition to the *Air Service News Letter* piece, she spoke with the African American weekly the *California Eagle*, and claimed to be twenty-three years old, rather than her accurate age of thirty-one. In the same interview she claimed to have flown in six European countries, when in fact she had only flown in three.

She also gave an interview to the African-American weekly *Dallas Express* in which she said she had changed her plans from opening a school in Northern California to opening a school in the Los Angeles area.

The press generally loved Coleman and printed her statements without question, but one article from the Baltimore *Afro-American* (which J. A. Jackson wrote for) probed Coleman's ability to fly a sustained, long-distance flight. There was no author credited for the article, though some suspect it was Jackson. Whomever the writer was, he weakened his credibility by challenging Coleman to fly the 80 miles (129 km) from Los Angeles to San Francisco in an hour. In reality, the two cities are more than 400 miles (644 km) apart.

A Catastrophic Crash

With her JN-4 assembled and ready, Coleman set out to perform on February 4, 1923, at the new Palomar Park fairgrounds. Ten thousand people were in attendance, and Coleman was excited to fly an exhibition in her new plane—the first one she had ever owned.

Unfortunately, Bessie Coleman never made it to the show. She started off from an airport in Santa Monica, 25 miles (40 km) away. When she took off to fly to the fairgrounds, the plane's motor stalled at 300 feet (91.5 meters). The plane smashed into the ground, with Coleman unconscious in the wreckage. She regained consciousness for long enough to ask the doctor on site to get her patched up so she could make it to the air show for her fans, but it was apparent that would not be happening. Coleman had a broken leg, three broken ribs, multiple facial lacerations, and potential internal injuries.

The crowd was angry that Coleman missed the performance, and some demanded refunds, despite the unavoidable change in plans. Coleman was undaunted. From the hospital, she sent a telegram asking her friends and well wishers to tell fans that as soon as she could walk again, she would be flying again.

Coleman knew the risks of her career. In the two weeks preceding her accident, five pilots were killed in three separate accidents that had similar circumstances to Coleman's (engine failure after takeoff). As the *Afro-American* reported in February 1923, Coleman said in a lecture, "I am anxious to teach some of you [African Americans] to fly, for accidents may happen. I may drift out and there would be someone to take my place."

Coleman was in the hospital for three months, and in that time she continued to work toward her dream of running an aviation school for people of color. She even placed a notice in the *California Eagle* offering a contract to the Coleman School of Aeronautics. She was recruiting students even though she didn't yet have any planes or an actual school. The contract required students to pay an advance of $400 toward their tuition, and it's thought that Coleman planned to use these advances to fund the startup of her school. As she continued to recuperate outside of the hospital, she gave lectures at the YMCA to earn more funds for her school. Still, all this fundraising wasn't yet enough to make the school a reality, and in June 1923, she returned to Chicago with a little money, but no school and no planes.

Back to Chicago

Coleman's luck didn't change much for the better when she returned to Chicago. She booked a major exhibition in Columbus, Ohio, that was rained out. She did perform at the rescheduled show a week later, but the media didn't give it much coverage. She planned a tour through the South that didn't pan out, partly due to broken contracts and Coleman's constant stream of ever-changing managers.

Coleman took a break for a while and spent time with family and friends. In the evenings, she went to events on The Stroll; sometimes with an escort on her arm, even though she was still technically married to her husband, Claude. For eighteen months she spent time in Chicago, in the meantime searching for a role in an air circus or anything that would bring her back to flying and potentially realize her dream of owning an aviation school. Finally, she found an opportunity in Texas, giving lectures and performing exhibition flights.

A Return to Texas and the Skies

By now, it was spring of 1925, more than two years since Coleman's California accident that landed her in the hospital for three months. Still introducing herself to the press as a twenty-three-year-old with a college degree who had trained in flight in numerous European countries, Coleman set up her home base in Houston.

Coleman's triumphant return to the skies was scheduled for June 19, 1925, Juneteenth. An exuberant Coleman performed stalls, dives, barrel rolls, figure eights, and loops in a borrowed plane. Spectators had the opportunity to go up for airplane

Coleman poses on one of the planes she flew, circa 1920.

rides afterward. The event was wildly successful. On June 27, 1925, the *Houston Informer*, a black newspaper, called the affair "the first time colored public of the South ha[d] been given the opportunity to fly" and said the public "[clamored] for another [chance to do so] soon." The event was such a triumph that Coleman was quickly booked for two more shows in Houston, and one in Richmond, Texas.

Coleman used her success in Texas to her advantage and appealed to African American women to learn how to fly. By this point, she had figured out that to make strides toward equality for blacks in the field of aviation, women needed to be more involved. It seemed white men saw African American men as a threat but were more willing to accept women. Coleman began appealed to black women to do as she had done, and to take an interest in aviation and prove that the skies could be filled with people of any color.

More Than a Pilot

Coleman continued to perform in air shows while in Texas, but more and more she was turning to lecturing to make money. It was expensive to arrange for planes and participate in air shows, but it was virtually free to lecture, so she had a much better profit margin. She had plenty of material for her lectures, and she had also collected a lot of film footage of her flights, which attendees enjoyed seeing.

Coleman traveled to Dallas to give a lecture and reportedly perform in an air show, though there is no indication that the air show ever actually happened. She did give her lecture at the Ella B. Moore Theater, and she spent time at Love Field airport. While there, she looked for a plane to purchase. She found a JN-4 she liked. Coleman didn't have enough money to buy it outright, but she arranged to make payments on it. It was in need of repair, anyway, so waiting a while to take possession of it wasn't a problem. Coleman moved on to her next location, Wharton, Texas, where she added another skill to her repertoire: parachuting.

Liza Dilworth, an African American woman who had jumped from Coleman's plane at a show in San Antonio, was supposed to jump in Wharton, but she backed out. Coleman, not wanting

Expanding Opportunities for Women

Although Bessie Coleman's job opportunities were limited, even in Chicago, for white women there were more options. Between about 1880 and 1930, Chicago experienced a great deal of growth in the career opportunities available to women. The Illinois Bureau of Labor Statistics was created, with Florence Kelley at its helm as chief factory inspector. She hired five female deputies to work with her. Nursing and social work jobs were plentiful, as were teaching and librarian positions. Many women flocked to office jobs as stenographers, typists, and telephone operators, too. For those who wanted to further their career opportunities, journalism, law, and medical schools began to open their doors to women. If Bessie Coleman had been a white woman, she would have had quite a few possible avenues for employment. However she had to contend with discrimination based not only her gender but also her ethnicity.

to disappoint her fans, decided that she'd hire a pilot to fly the plane and do the jump herself. Like most everything else, Coleman proved to be a success at parachuting. She jumped from an altitude of 3,000 feet (914.5 meters) and landed in the center of the crowd, winning rave reviews from white reporters on the scene.

Coleman did numerous other shows in Texas, including in Waxahachie, her childhood home. It was a triumph for the laundress and sharecropper's daughter to return to her hometown a celebrity.

The End of an Era

After her tour in Texas, Coleman returned home to Chicago to spend time with her family. While there, she worked with an agent she sometimes used, D. Ireland Thomas, to set up a speaking and exhibition tour of the South. It was to commence right after Christmas.

Coleman spent Christmas Eve with her sister, Elois Patterson, who said in her memoir of Coleman, "We had a joyful Christmas Eve. We made and wrapped Christmas presents and I hemmed a black taffeta dress of hers. We cooked, tasted, and drank coffee and chatted the whole night through. All of a sudden it was broad daylight and time for Bessie to leave." Little did Elois know, that would be the last time she saw her sister.

Coleman began her tour in Savannah, Georgia, and traveled around the state for lectures and interviews (and one missed air show, likely because she couldn't find anyone to borrow a plane from). She then moved on to do more lectures in Florida. She spent a few months in Florida, staying at the church parsonage of the Mount Zion Missionary Baptist

Institutional Church in Orlando. The reverend of the church was a man named Hezekiah Hill. He and his wife, Viola, took an interest in Coleman, who had been religious as a child but who had gradually fallen away from the church. Coleman became a born-again Christian with Viola's guidance. Coleman was remembered fondly by the children in the Hills' neighborhood. Jessie Lee Green, a neighborhood child, said in an April 1991 interview, "She was a friendly lady, talking to everyone, even us children. She couldn't get rid of us. We admired everything about her, especially her driving airplanes ... The last time I saw her she had on her uniform. She was smiling. She had beautiful short hair and a beautiful personality."

Viola Hill wanted very much for Coleman to stop stunt flying. It was a dangerous pastime, and Viola encouraged Coleman to raise the money for her aviation school by continuing to do lectures and perhaps opening a beauty shop in Orlando. Coleman took Viola's words to heart, but she couldn't set aside her love of flying.

When Coleman met Edwin M. Beeman, heir to the Beeman Chewing Gum fortune, it seemed like the break she had long been waiting for. The exact nature of Coleman and Beeman's association is unknown—an interracial relationship in that era in Florida would not have been accepted by most of society. Whatever the connection was, Beeman agreed to finance the remaining amount due on the plane Coleman had picked out at Love Field.

Coleman left the Hills, Beeman, and Orlando behind on April 27, 1926, and headed to Jacksonville, Florida, where her plane would be delivered. In Jacksonville, the publicity chairman of the Negro Welfare League, John Thomas Betsch, met Coleman. He had scheduled several lectures for her, as

Curtiss JN-4 Jenny

While Bessie Coleman learned to fly on a Nieuport Type 82, in America the common training plane for that era was the Curtiss JN-4 Jenny. It was manufactured starting in 1915 by the Curtiss Aeroplane Company in New York and was used as a training plane for pilots in the United States Army. In fact, it's estimated that 95 percent of World War I pilots trained on a Jenny.

After World War I, it was used as a civilian aircraft, and surplus military planes were sold at low prices to aviation enthusiasts. In total, 6,813 Jennys were built between 1915 and the early 1920s.

Bessie Coleman bought two planes of her own, both Jennys. Unfortunately, both of them crashed shortly after she bought them—one due to engine failure, and one due to a maintenance issue.

well as an exhibition at the Negro Welfare League's Field Day, to be held a few days later on May 1.

Meanwhile, William D. Wills, a white mechanic from Love Field, was flying Coleman's new Jenny to Jacksonville. The plane had had maintenance done to it, but clearly not enough. It malfunctioned twice during the flight from Dallas to Jacksonville, and Wills had to make two emergency landings en route. Two local pilots met Wills when he landed in Jacksonville. They later commented that Wills was an excellent pilot but that they were surprised the plane had made it from Dallas because its engine was very worn and poorly maintained.

On April 30, 1926, Coleman and Wills went up in the plane for a test flight. Coleman had planned a jump for the exhibition, and she wanted to pick a suitable spot for it. She sat in the rear cockpit and left her seatbelt off because she was too short to peer over the edge of the cockpit if her seatbelt was fastened. Wills and Coleman were cruising at 3,500 feet (1067 m), going roughly 80 miles per hour (129 kmh), when the plane suddenly gained speed to 110 miles per hour (177 kmh) and went into a nose dive. According to those watching the flight, at about 1,000 feet (305 m), the plane went into a tailspin, and at 500 feet (152 m), it flipped upside down, dumping Coleman out. She died on impact. Witnesses reported that she somersaulted end over end through the air before she hit the ground at full force, reportedly breaking almost every bone in her body.

Wills was killed in the accident, too. He was unable to regain control of the plane, and two people who witnessed the crash tried to lift the plane off his body but were unable. A police officer at the scene lit a cigarette, and the match ignited gasoline fumes from the plane, sending the aircraft up in flames. It's unknown whether Wills died in the crash or in the subsequent fire. The fire and the looters who stripped the plane after the fact left little evidence, but there was one key piece that led officials to determine the cause of the crash: a wrench that had either come loose from a fitting or that had accidentally been left in the engine slid into the control gears and jammed them.

Had Wills and Coleman been piloting a newer plane, the accident likely would not have happened; newer models had gear coverings that would have prevented it. Tragically, Coleman had bought the plane she could afford, and unfortunately that may have played a large role in her early death.

Although the African American community heavily mourned Coleman's death, the white press largely ignored it. The *Florida Times Union* and the *Jacksonville Journal* both covered the crash, but they focused almost exclusively on the death of Wills. One stated that Wills was teaching Coleman how to fly and only mentioned her twice, devoting the entire rest of the article to Wills. The other paper only used her name once, focused most of the story on Wills, and referred to Coleman in all other mentions as simply "the woman."

It was a sad end for a woman who did so much to further opportunity for African Americans. Coleman may not have endeared herself to everyone, but there is no denying she became an inspiration to many.

four

Coleman's Achievements

"I thought it was my duty to risk my life to learn aviating and to encourage flying among men and women of the Race." —Bessie Coleman

As discussed, Bessie Coleman started her life in a one-room cabin with a dirt floor. She grew up the daughter of sharecroppers and was largely raised by a single mother after her father left the family. As a child, she vowed, "to amount to something." She faced poverty and racism growing up as an African American in the Jim Crow South. Additionally, Coleman grew up a woman in an era completely

Opposite: Bessie Coleman's pilot's license from the Fédération Aéronautique Internationale

dominated by men. Yet somehow, she accomplished much in her thirty-four years and went on to make history, becoming an American legend.

The First African American and Native American Aviatrix

Coleman's major accomplishment was earning her pilot's license. When Coleman set her sights on becoming a pilot, the United States didn't require pilots to be licensed. It was the early days of flight, and things were very informal. If you had a plane (or could borrow one) and learned to fly, you could consider yourself a pilot. However, this unofficial luxury only applied to white men.

Coleman, on the other hand, was a woman descended from Native Americans and African American slaves—two groups that did not have equal legal rights to whites until the early twentieth century. Pilots tended to be a less judgmental group than others, but the fact still remained that Coleman was both female and black, so without a license she would be unlikely to get anyone to let her fly. Each time Coleman tried to find someone in the United States to teach her to fly, she came up empty handed. No one would agree to teach a black woman to fly a plane.

Even once she traveled across the Atlantic Ocean to France, where she thought racism and sexism were not as prevalent, it was not easy for her to find acceptance. The first flight schools Coleman approached turned her down. She ultimately found a spot in France's acclaimed École d'Aviation des Frères Caudron at Le Crotoy, and she set aside any fears and reservations and plunged herself into the study of flight and aeronautics. The result was that on June 15, 1921, Coleman became the first woman of African American and Native American descent to earn a pilot's license. What's more, she was the first person—male or female—of African American and Native American descent to earn an international pilot's license from the Fédération Aéronautique Internationale. This distinction meant she was the only person of African American or Native American descent to be licensed to fly anywhere in the world.

Without achieving that distinction, Coleman's life might have been little more than a reference in the local obituaries upon her death. Yet with that license, Coleman became a sensation and will be forever known as the first African American female pilot.

An Inspiration

Coleman was not one for record setting. She didn't aspire to be the fastest pilot or to set records for the longest distance flown. She wanted to be recognized and to inspire other African Americans to pursue flight. Rather than spending her time trying to set or break records, Coleman spent her time actively participating in air shows and exhibitions, lecturing, and raising both money and awareness so that she could motivate other African Americans to follow in her footsteps. Thus, her life reads as a progression of small successes all working toward her goals of making a name for herself and inspiring other African Americans to do the same.

It is also the tale of a person who refused to take no for an answer, though she said no herself many times. No, she did not want a life of sharecropping. No, she did not aspire

Coleman receives flowers from an aeronautical instructor in 1922 at Curtiss Field, Garden City, Long Island.

to be a laundress or other domestic worker. No, she did not care to get married for the sole purpose of starting a family. No, she would not give up on her dream of flying, even when no one in the United States would teach her. No, she would not stop working to open an aviation school for people of all ethnicities, religions, and backgrounds.

Coleman said no to what she refused to accept—and refused to hear no from those who didn't believe she could or should accomplish it. When she couldn't earn money for her aeronautical education in one way, she turned to another source. When she couldn't earn enough money to open her school simply by doing exhibition flights, she came up with other ideas to help her gain the funds she needed.

All of Coleman's many individual small accomplishments—finding the funds to go to France to learn to fly, getting booked at air shows and exhibitions across the nation, getting booked at lectures when she wasn't flying, purchasing her own airplanes—were stepping stones to a larger goal of driving change and are evidence of how she lived her life. Coleman was a performer at heart, and she loved to tell a good story about herself. Yet underneath that bluster and showmanship was a determined woman who kept pushing toward her goals.

Coleman's impact was not just as a pilot in the skies but also as an activist on the ground. She helped break down the color barrier in the field of aeronautics, not only by being an African American aviatrix—though certainly she did that—but also by refusing to allow segregation at shows where she performed.

When Coleman was performing in the early 1900s, the United States was still very segregated. In many places (particularly in the South), blacks could not eat at the same restaurants as whites, drink from the same drinking fountains, use the same restrooms, or even ride in the same train cars. Nevertheless, Coleman refused to allow this sort of segregation at the air shows where she performed.

In 1925, when Coleman was on a tour of Texas, she was scheduled to perform at an air show in Waxahachie, the small Texas city where she had grown up. It was the very place where she'd had to walk more than 4 miles (6.4 km) from the black side of town to the white side of town twice a week to collect and deliver laundry to the wealthier white homeowners—a place where Coleman undoubtedly felt keenly the sting of racism and segregation. When the show organizers announced that the show would allow both blacks and whites to attend

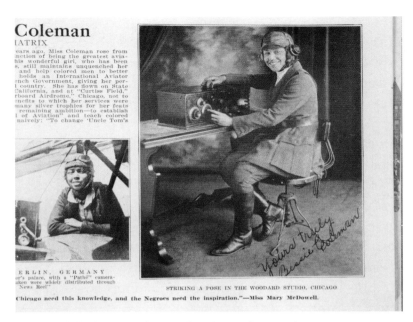

Coleman

IATRIX

ears ago, Miss Coleman rose from
nction of being the greatest avia-
his wonderful girl, who has been
s, still maintains unquenched her
and help colored men to better
holds an International Aviator
ench Government, giving her per-
l country. She has flown on State
California, and at "Curtiss Field,"
rboard Airdrome," Chicago, not to
nefits to which her services were
many silver trophies for her feats
remaining ambition—to establish
l of Aviation" and teach colored
naively: "To change 'Uncle Tom's

ERLIN, GERMANY
er's palace, with a "Pathé" camera-
aken were which distributed through
News Reel"

STRIKING A POSE IN THE WOODARD STUDIO, CHICAGO

Chicago need this knowledge, and the Negroes need the inspiration."—Miss Mary McDowell.

A media darling, Coleman has been featured in numerous books and articles.

but that the two groups would have separate areas and would have to enter through separate gates, Coleman put down her foot and refused to perform. The organizers eventually agreed that blacks and whites could use the same entrance gates, though they insisted that the races had to be separated once inside the grounds where the show was being held.

At that point, Coleman needed the income from the show to help her purchase a plane so she could continue working toward her goal of opening up an aviation school. So reluctantly, Coleman acquiesced. She still wasn't thrilled with the situation, but she at least had the victory of having blacks and whites use a common entrance gate. She had won an important battle, even if not the war.

Coleman challenged the system yet again in Florida in 1926. She was scheduled to perform a parachute jump in Orlando, but when she learned it was a whites-only event, she announced that unless the show's organizers changed the rule, she would send her plane back to Texas and withdraw from the show. It worked, and the organizers allowed blacks into the show. Amusingly, Coleman was somewhat bluffing. She may indeed have refused to participate in the show if the organizers hadn't changed their rule, but she had no plane to send back to Texas—she was planning to borrow one for the show!

Supporters

In later years, Coleman had a reputation for being difficult or erratic to work with. She went through multiple managers and did not always follow through on her agreements. Nonetheless, she did have those who were largely loyal to her, respected her ambition, and supported her endeavors. It is worth revisiting two individuals whose support was instrumental to Coleman.

Robert Abbott

Robert Abbott was born on November 24, 1879, in Georgia and came from a long line of strong, proud black women. His mother was a noted benefactor of black schools; two of his aunts founded Episcopal churches in Atlanta, Georgia; and his cousin was a university student in Washington, DC. Bessie Coleman had admired Abbott, who was well known on the South Side not just as the founder of the *Chicago Defender* but also as an advocate of social justice for African Americans. Given how vocal Abbott was in encouraging black people to pursue their dreams, it was natural for Coleman to approach him for advice when she could find no one willing to teach her how to fly.

As mentioned, Abbott was the person who encouraged Coleman to try her luck overseas, and he offered to provide Coleman with a letter of recommendation for French aviation schools if she could learn French and save the money to go. Without the financial assistance she received from a few benefactors such as Abbott, she likely would not have been able to make the journey. This wasn't pure altruism on Abbott's part. He believed in Coleman and wanted her to succeed, but he also wanted to sell newspapers and continue to spread motivational stories to other African Americans. If Coleman achieved her goals, she would certainly be the perfect example of a black person moving north and fighting for equal opportunities.

It was a relationship that worked well for several years, since Coleman was all too happy to play media darling to gain exposure for her future aviation school. When she returned to Chicago from France in October 1921, Coleman gave interviews for the *Defender* and detailed her experiences while learning to fly in France. Like other media outlets, the *Defender* took Coleman at her word and printed her stories as she told them. Some of them were true, and some were embellished.

When Coleman decided she needed to return to Europe to further her flying skills, Abbott helped her once again. She spent a week in New York City before leaving for France, and Abbott arranged for William White, manager of the New York headquarters of the *Defender*, to act as her agent. After her second stint in Europe, Coleman returned to the United States once again. Abbott had the *Defender* staff in New York arrange an air show for her, which turned out to be the first public flight of an African American woman in the United States. Although postponed a week from its original date due to rain, it still drew a few thousand spectators, thanks in part to the *Defender*'s heavy publicizing.

Abbott again scheduled an air show for Coleman when she returned to Chicago in the early fall of 1922. By this point, Coleman had earned the distinction of being considered a socialite in the *Defender*. The paper covered her social engagements, such as when a luncheon was given in her honor. Just as the *Defender* had done for Coleman's New York City show, they highly publicized her Chicago performance, saying in October 1922 that Coleman had "amazed continental Europe and been applauded in Paris, Berlin and Munich" and giving lavish descriptions of the show Coleman would put on for the Chicago audience. The publicity was enough to entice more than two thousand spectators to the Chicago show.

In time, Abbott's interest in Coleman waned. The negative publicity for breaking a film contract and for quickly cycling through several managers tarnished her reputation. Additionally, her serious crash in Southern California left her in the hospital for months. Coleman was no longer selling papers in a good way. There was no reported falling out between Abbott and Coleman. Perhaps he was simply only interested in people with stories of black empowerment, and unfortunately Coleman's story no longer fit the bill.

Viola Tillinghast Hill

Another major supporter of Coleman's was Viola Tillinghast Hill. She and her husband, the Reverend Hezekiah Keith Hill, were African American community activists in Orlando,

Artist Michael Hogue paid tribute to Coleman with this color illustration.

Florida. Coleman had gone to Orlando near the beginning of her tour of the South in the 1920s, and she immediately connected with the Hills. The Hills invited her to stay at the parsonage of Reverend Hill's church, and she became so close with them that she referred to them as Mother and Daddy. With their tutelage, she became a born-again Christian.

Viola disapproved of Coleman performing in air shows as a stunt flyer because it was dangerous, so she encouraged Coleman to give up stunt flying and instead focus on doing lectures and teaching students to raise money for her aviation school. She also suggested that Coleman open a beauty shop to help bring in more money, since she knew the costs associated with starting an aviation school would be high.

Coleman appears to have taken Viola's advice to an extent. Elois Patterson recalled a 1926 letter from her sister, in which Coleman wrote, "I am right on the threshold of opening a school." She had even acquired a rattan chair that she planned to use in her beauty shop. When Coleman left Orlando to travel to Jacksonville to finally take possession of a plane she had bought in Texas and to then perform in an air show, she promised Viola that when she returned to Orlando, she would no longer do stunts. She would lecture and teach, as

Viola had suggested. She also told Viola that she was happier than she had ever been in her life, thanks in part to the Hills' friendship and support. Unfortunately, Coleman couldn't keep her promise to Viola because the trip to Jacksonville was her last.

Foes and Detractors

While Coleman had supporters in people like Viola Hill, Robert Abbott, and her large extended family, she also had her share of detractors. Coleman was unique in her convictions and refusal to conform to the expectations of other people. Some were intimidated by her confidence, as she lived in an era when African Americans were held in lower regard than white people and when many in society believed black women should be submissive to their husbands.

Perhaps surprisingly, some of the critics Coleman faced were African American men. An editorial in the black weekly *Amsterdam News* called "Colored Women Venturing Too Far From Children, Kitchen, Clothes and Church" slammed independent black women like Coleman, saying that women's "biological function … is to bear and rear children" and saw the rise of black women working outside the home instead of having many children as "race suicide." The editorial claimed the "liberalization of women must always be kept within the boundary fixed by nature." Coleman was untroubled by claims like these. She was wholly focused on her goal of empowering African Americans to fly, and by this time she had decided that she ought to focus her efforts on African American women.

If one person could be considered Coleman's foe, it would be *Billboard* writer J. A. Jackson, a black writer for a white

A Contemporary: Amelia Earhart

Amelia Earhart is probably the United States' best-known aviatrix from the early twentieth century, so it is reasonable to assume that Bessie Coleman and Amelia Earhart might have been acquainted. That, however, would not be true. Amelia Earhart was white and Bessie Coleman was black, and thus they did not move in the same social circles. Even though they were both groundbreaking women in a brand-new, male-dominated field, societal expectations dictated that the color of their skin keep them separate.

The two women did have some parallels in the field, though. Around the time Bessie Coleman went to Northern California to meet with the Coast Tire and Rubber Company to discuss doing some publicity for them, Amelia Earhart was endorsing airplane builders and flying an actress around in exhibition flights to help her boost her celebrity. Both women were clearly business minded, and it's entirely possible that one or both was inspired by the other in that respect.

Amelia Earhart, the first female pilot to fly solo across the Atlantic Ocean, disappeared in 1937.

Air shows were popular with blacks and whites, but they were typically segregated in the Jim Crow South.

publication. He started out as Coleman's supporter, writing positive reviews about her performances. Coleman generally struggled to get attention in the white press, so Jackson's praise was certainly welcome. All that would change when Coleman walked off the set of the proposed feature film *Shadow and Sunshine*. Jackson had recommended her for the role and was furious that Coleman would break the contract. He began writing caustic stories about her. He made jabs about her poor upbringing in Waxahachie and maintained that she did not have the gentility of others in the industry.

The broken film contract was not the only reason Jackson was angry. As part of the National Association of Colored Fairs, Jackson had helped arrange for Coleman to perform at fairs in both Virginia and North Carolina. Coleman didn't attend either fair, leaving Jackson, along with all the others who had worked to secure her performance, looking rather silly.

Jackson continued to write negative pieces about Coleman, asserting she lacked professionalism and refinement. He wrote about her going through three managers in five months, even though some weren't officially managers. There were also a few uncredited newspaper pieces in which the writing style bears a striking similarity of Jackson's, and it has been postulated that Jackson was behind those as well.

The Woman Who Wouldn't Be Grounded

Bessie Coleman refused to accept defeat, even when she nearly lost her life. When she crashed her plane in California in 1923, the accident could very easily have ended Coleman's life. However, from her hospital bed, where she lay with a full-leg cast, three broken ribs, and a hugely swollen face, Coleman sent a telegram to her friends and fans: "TELL THEM ALL THAT AS SOON AS I CAN WALK I'M GOING TO FLY! AND MY FAITH IN AVIATION AND THE [USE] IT WILL SERVE IN FULFILLING THE DESTINY OF MY PEOPLE ISN'T SHAKEN AT ALL."

Coleman's body may have been damaged, but certainly her courage was intact!

five

Coleman's Legacy

"Aviation is just beginning its period of growth, and if we get into it now, while it is still uncrowded, we can grow as aviation grows."
—William J. Powell

B essie Coleman's contributions to the field of aviation are both enormous and modest. Although she did not invent any sort of new aviation technology, nor set any records, she did break social conventions and boundaries.

Opposite: Coleman inspired many future female aviators, like helicopter pilot L'Shanda Holmes, to take to the skies.

She was a female African American and Native American pilot in a time when opportunities both in the skies and on the ground were dominated by white men. Her legacy has certainly touched the field of aviation permanently, and she assuredly inspired others to fight for their dreams. Many African Americans followed in her wake to become pilots—including Coleman's own nephew!

An Inspired Nephew: Arthur Freeman

One of the spectators when Coleman flew her exhibition flight in Chicago was none other than her eight-year-old nephew, Arthur Freeman, son of Coleman's younger sister Nilus. In a 1983 interview with Philip S. Hart, Arthur recalled seeing his

Pioneers like Coleman paved the way for pilots such as Vernice Armour, the first African American combat pilot in the United States.

aunt perform in Chicago and thinking, "My aunt's a flier! ... And she's just beautiful wearing that long leather coat over her uniform and the leather helmet with aviator goggles! That's my aunt! A real live aviator!"

Freeman took that admiration and turned it into his own dream. He received the Soldier's Medal as a sergeant in the Tuskegee Army Flying School. Freeman was one of the famed Tuskegee Airmen, the first African American aviators in the United States Army. He ended up being part of the all-black maintenance team for the army's 477th Bombardment Group.

Equality in the Military: Willa Beatrice Brown and Vernice Armour

While Bessie Coleman became the first licensed African American aviatrix, she had to go to France to do so. In 1936, about a decade after Coleman's death, Willa Brown became the first black woman to obtain a pilot's license and mechanic's license in the United States. Soon after, she helped found and manage the National Airmen Association of America, whose mission was to earn African Americans the right to fly in the military.

Willa Brown was an advocate for gender and racial equality both in flight and in the military. Brown worked to open the Civilian Pilot Training Program up to African Americans, a move instrumental in the formation of the Tuskegee Airmen, and she became the head of the CPTP in Chicago. She was also active in the Civil Aeronautics Authority and the Women's Advisory Board of the **FAA**. Brown is also known as the first

African American woman to run for US Congress, and the first African American officer in the US Civil Air Patrol.

Vernice Armour earned her wings in 2001 as the first African American female naval aviator in the Marine Corps. In 2003, she flew her first mission as the first female African American combat pilot for the US Armed Forces. She flew the AH-1W SuperCobra attack helicopter for the HMLA-169 unit during the Iraq War.

Commercial Pilots: Janet Bragg and Jill E. Brown Hiltz

Willa Brown and Bessie Coleman both had their private pilot's licenses, but Janet Bragg was the first African American woman to hold a commercial pilot's license. She was the first African American woman to enroll at the Curtiss Wright School of Aeronautics in Coleman's home city of Chicago in 1928. She also enrolled at Aeronautical University in 1933, where she was the only woman among twenty-four African American men in the program at the segregated school. After being turned down at various institutions because of her race, Janet completed the Civilian Pilot Training Program at Tuskegee.

In the 1970s, Jill E. Brown Hiltz broke another barrier in the aviation world when she became the first African American woman to be hired as a pilot for a major US airline. She earned her pilot's license at age seventeen, and at age twenty-four she became the first African American woman to join the United States Navy's flight training program. Four years later, she was hired as a pilot by Texas International Airlines.

Although Janet Bragg held a commercial pilot's license in the earlier half of the twentieth century and Jill Brown Hiltz was a pilot for a major US airline in the 1970s, it wasn't until 1994 that an African American woman was made a commercial airline captain. As recently as the 1980s, Patrice Clarke Washington, an African American woman from the Bahamas who wanted to fly commercial planes, was denied the opportunity because of her ethnicity and gender. However, she prevailed and started flying as a first office for the United Parcel Service (UPS), where she was later promoted to captain.

African American Male Aviators

Although Bessie Coleman focused much of her recruitment efforts on black women, based on her belief they were more likely to be willing to challenge the racial barriers than men, she did encourage African American men to fly as well. In fact, in an essay about Coleman published by the Smithsonian National Air and Space Museum, her sister Elois recalls, "I remember one letter she wrote me saying she had taken an escort, and even went to a pool room, so determined was she to have Negro men become air-minded."

Coleman didn't live long enough to train all that many students, but her success in the air helped pave the way for a long line of African American male aviators. Unbeknownst to many, the first African American aviator in the United States was Emory Malick, who earned his license in 1912, before Coleman. Yet his distinction was not revealed by historians until 2004!

Instead, for years it was thought that James Herman Banning, who earned his pilot's license in 1926, was the first licensed African American aviator in the United States. Banning was also the first African American pilot to fly coast to coast, a feat he achieved in 1932 along with copilot and mechanic

Equality in the Skies Today?

Bessie Coleman paved the way for future African American aviators as well as future female aviators. Over ninety years have passed since Coleman's death, and as it turns out, there are still inequalities. As of 2015, there were an estimated 130,000 licensed commercial airline pilots worldwide. Although the breakdown by gender is constantly shifting, as of 2016 only an estimated 5,000 of those pilots were women, or about 4 percent. When you consider airline pilots only in the United States, the rate of female pilots is about 5 percent of 53,000 pilots for major and regional airlines. Breaking it down by ethnicity, according to the FAA in 2013, only 2 percent of licensed pilots in the United States identified as African American.

Why the low numbers nearly a century after Bessie Coleman proved that a black woman could fly? It seems that many still stereotype the role of commercial pilot as a career for a white man. Patrick Smith, who wrote a book about air travel called *Cockpit Confidential*, cites the fact that for decades many pilots were military fliers, and most military pilots were white men.

Judy Cameron, Air Canada's first female pilot, faced this sexism even from other women. In a 2015 interview, Cameron recounted how a female reporter in the 1970s once asked her how she could fly while dealing with premenstrual syndrome. Cameron also reported that a man once noticed her in her pilot's uniform and commented, "Huh, a woman pilot. Well, at least it keeps them off the roads."

The discrimination extends to African American pilots as well. In 2014, Michael Zirulnik, a reporter covering the lack

While black female pilots are still few in number, women like Demetria Elosiebo, the first black female rotary-wing pilot in the Army National Guard, do exist.

of diversity in airline pilots, stated that a captain at a large regional airline had said his company wouldn't hire African American pilots because "they drop out of training or quit after a year." The same reporter said the human resources director of an air cargo transport company told him that she was told to hire an African American female pilot to fulfill the company's diversity requirements, but that after that her boss told her to never hire another African American female pilot again because things were "gonna stay the way they've always been around there."

Bessie Coleman may have broken barriers to become the first African American and Native American aviatrix, but it is clear there is still more work to be done toward equality.

Thomas C. Allen. Like Bessie Coleman, Banning died young, at age thirty-two, his life cut short in a plane crash.

One young man whom Coleman inspired was William J. Powell, an African American man who served in World War I and then returned home to Chicago. Like Coleman, Powell found that most aviators in the United States were unwilling to

William J. Powell (*right*), shown here with Hubert Julian, a parachute jumper, cited Coleman as an inspiration and had similar goals of enabling African Americans to fly.

train him. Also like Coleman, Powell channeled that frustration into a dream of opening a flight school. Whereas Coleman wanted to open a flight school for all, Powell envisioned one specifically for African Americans. Their goals differed slightly but still had the same core vision: enabling African Americans to fly. As Powell stated in *Black Wings*, a fictionalized account of his life that he published in 1934 and dedicated to Bessie Coleman, "There is a better job and a better future in aviation for Negroes than in any other industry, and the reason is this: aviation is just beginning its period of growth, and if we get into it now, while it is still uncrowded, we can grow as aviation grows."

Unlike Coleman, however, Powell ultimately found a school in the United States that would train him, and he moved to Southern California to attend the Los Angeles School of Flight. In the early 1930s, Powell established the Bessie Coleman Aero Club to promote aviation awareness among the black community. At the time, only 12 African American pilots existed among the 18,041 licensed pilots in the United States, and many commercial airlines wouldn't even allow African Americans to fly as passengers on their planes. The club sponsored the first all-black air show in 1931, which drew approximately 15,000 attendees. The club was technically open to all, although most members were indeed African American.

Powell was tireless in his efforts to "fill the air with black wings." In addition to his book and the Bessie Coleman Aero Club, he made a film about an African American man who aspired to be a pilot. He also published the *Craftsmen Aero-News*, which covered topics in African American aviation. He entreated black celebrities such as jazz musician Duke Ellington and boxer Joe Louis to support and donate to his cause, and

Beyond the Sky

When Bessie Coleman was dreaming big, the sky was as far as one could imagine. To soar among the birds was so novel that it almost defied imagination for many! But forty years after Coleman's death, Americans were dreaming even bigger—they were reaching for the stars. One such American was a young woman named Sally Ride, who joined the National Aeronautics and Space Administration (NASA) in 1978 and became the first American woman in space when she was a member of the support crew aboard the space shuttle *Challenger* in 1983. The **USSR** had sent two women into space already, but the United States hadn't—just as Bessie Coleman found, the United States was a bit behind the times in terms of gender discrimination.

Bessie Coleman reached for the skies, which enabled women like Sally Ride to reach beyond, for the stars.

he offered scholarships and technical training in aeronautics to young African Americans who were interested in the field.

William J. Powell was forty-five when he died in 1942. The cause was thought to be a result of exposure to toxic gas when he served in World War I.

No doubt, all of the African American pilots who came after Bessie Coleman owe a debt of gratitude to the woman who proved that a black woman could fly a plane every bit as capably as her white male counterparts. Likewise, all aviatrixes owe a similar debt of gratitude to Coleman. There were a few other female pilots when Coleman was flying, and indeed they were inspiring, but they were few and far between, so any woman who fought to fly in the 1920s stands as a pioneer who helped open doors for the women who came after her.

Glossary

barnstormer A person who performs aeronautical stunt shows in rural areas.

Black Belt An area in Chicago's South Side that was composed of primarily African American neighborhoods in the early 1900s.

cabinet The most senior officers of the executive branch of the US federal government—it includes the vice president and the heads of fifteen executive departments.

dirigible An airship with a rigid structure, often resembling a blimp.

disenfranchise To deprive a person of the right to vote or exercise another privilege.

Emancipation Proclamation An executive order signed by President Abraham Lincoln that declared three million slaves to be free citizens.

FAA Federal Aviation Administration; the authority that regulates civil aviation in the United States.

homeowners' association HOA; a board that provides upkeep for a certain neighborhood and enforces a set of rules and regulations that homeowners in that neighborhood are required to follow.

involuntary servitude The act of a person laboring against his or her will to benefit another person.

Jim Crow laws Local and state laws that enforced racial segregation in the Southern United States.

Juneteenth June 19, the day that African Americans celebrate as commemorating the end of slavery in the United States.

kaiser The ruler of Germany until the end of World War I.

monoplane An airplane with only one set of wings.

NAACP National Association for the Advancement of Colored People; a civil rights organization in the United States.

New Negroes Members of a movement in which African Americans refused to accept and submit to segregation and Jim Crow laws.

pitch The vertical angle of a plane during flight.

Reconstruction Era Roughly the decade after the Civil War, in which the United States (particularly the South) was transitioning from a system of slavery to an entirely free society.

USSR Union of Soviet Socialist Republics; a group of Eastern European and Eurasian countries that formed a socialist state. The USSR was dissolved in 1991.

yaw The side-to-side movement of a plane during flight.

Chronology

1892 Bessie Coleman is born in Atlanta, Texas.

1894 Coleman's family moves to Waxahachie, Texas.

1896 *Plessy v. Ferguson* upholds segregation and establishes the "separate but equal" doctrine. Coleman begins attending a segregated school in 1898.

1901 Bessie Coleman's father, George Coleman, leaves the family. Coleman's school attendance is sporadic because she must help care for her younger siblings while her mother works to support the family.

1903 The Wright brothers successfully pilot a powered, heavier-than-air flying machine and achieve sustained flight.

1904 Coleman is formally accepted into the Missionary Baptist Church.

1910 Coleman enrolls in the Colored Agricultural and Normal University in Langston, Oklahoma. She attends for just one term, until she runs out of money and must return to Waxahachie.

1914 World War I erupts in Europe. It lasts until 1918.

1915 Coleman leaves Waxahachie for Chicago, where she moves in with her brothers and finds work as a manicurist.

1917 Coleman marries Claude Glenn, though she keeps the fact hidden from her family and friends.

1919 Coleman decides to pursue her interest in aviation.

1920 Travels to France to attend flight school, having found no one willing to teach her in the United States.

1921 Earns her internationally recognized pilot's license. That same year, she returns to the United States.

1922 Travels back to Europe to undertake more flight training. She is filmed flying over the defeated kaiser's palace in Berlin. She later shows the footage at lectures to those interested in aviation. Upon returning to Chicago, she performs several exhibition flights, and breaks a movie contract, which earns her the wrath of several media personnel.

1923 Coleman leaves Chicago and in California purchases her first plane. She is severely injured when the plane she purchased crashes in Southern California; she spends three months in the hospital.

1925 After an eighteen-month hiatus in which she recovers from her accident and returns to Chicago to try to rebuild her career, Coleman secures work doing a series of lectures and exhibition flights in Texas.

1926 Coleman arrives in the Deep South to do a series of lectures and exhibition flights.

1926 Bessie Coleman is killed when her plane malfunctions and she falls to her death.

1995 The US Postal Service issues a stamp in Bessie Coleman's honor.

2017 In honor of her 125th birthday, Bessie Coleman is featured as a Google Doodle.

Further Information

Books

Jervis, Julie. *The World Beneath Their Wings: A New Millennium of Female Aviators*. San Mateo, CA: In Flight Publishing, 2006.

Merry, Lois K. *Women Military Pilots of World War II*. Jefferson, NC: McFarland, 2010.

Rich, Doris L. *Queen Bess: Daredevil Aviator*. Washington, DC: Smithsonian Institution Press, 1993.

Websites

Bessie Coleman
http://www.bessiecoleman.com
This website has several pages that include a history of Bessie Coleman's life and accomplishments.

The Official Website of Bessie Coleman
http://www.bessiecoleman.org
Another website dedicated to the life and accomplishments of Bessie Coleman; this is the official site.

Women in Aviation and Space History
https://airandspace.si.edu/explore-and-learn/topics/women-in-aviation
The Smithsonian National Air and Space Museum has a comprehensive website covering notable female aviators in air and space history.

Films

Campbell, Sandra P. *Follow Your Dreams: The Bessie Coleman Story.* Kansas City, MO: KCPT, 2001.

In this one-woman show, Sandra Campbell performs as Bessie Coleman and tells her story. Written and performed by Campbell, and taped in front of a live audience.

Bibliography

"Aviatrix Dies in Plane Crash." *Pittsburgh Courier*, May 8, 1926.

"Aviatrix Must Sign Life Away to Learn Trade." *Chicago Defender*, October 8, 1921.

Bloom, Laura Begley. "Why Aren't There More Female Airline Pilots? This High-Flying Woman Is Breaking Boundaries." *Forbes*, June 23, 2016. http://www.forbes.com/sites/laurabegleybloom/2016/06/23/why-arent-there-more-female-airline-pilots-this-high-flying-woman-is-breaking-boundaries/#7518f8513f96.

Britton, Karen Gerhardt, Fred C. Elliott, and E. A. Miller. "Cotton Culture." In *Handbook of Texas Online*. Accessed November 30, 2016. http://www.tshaonline.org/handbook/online/articles/afc03.

"Colored Women Venturing Too Far From Children, Kitchen, Clothes and Church." *Amsterdam News*, February 4, 1925.

Cooper, Charlie, and Ann Cooper. *Tuskegee's Heroes: Featuring the Aviation Art of Roy LaGrone*. London: Crestline Books, 2015.

De León, Arnoldo, and Robert A. Calvert. "Segregation." In *Handbook of Texas Online*. Accessed November 30, 2016. http://www.tshaonline.org/handbook/online/articles/pks01.

"Flying Circus Unusual Event to Be Repeated." *Houston Informer*, June 27, 1925.

Hart, Philip S. Interview with Arthur Freeman conducted September 1983.

"A History of Women in Industry." National Women's History Museum, 2007. https://www.nwhm.org/online-exhibits/industry/10.htm.

Layson, Hana, and Kenneth Warren. "Chicago and the Great Migration, 1915–1950." The Newberry, March 14–15, 2013. http://dcc.newberry.org/collections/chicago-and-the-great-migration.

O'Flahavan, Leslie. "African American Pioneers in Aviation, 1920–Present." Smithsonian National Air and Space Museum, 1999. https://airandspace.si.edu/files/pdf/explore-and-learn/teaching-posters/aviation.pdf.

Morris, Hugh. "Why Are There So Few Female Pilots?" *Telegraph*, October 27, 2015. http://www.telegraph.co.uk/travel/news/Why-are-there-so-few-female-pilots.

Plantz, Connie. *The Life of Bessie Coleman*. Berkeley Heights, NJ: Enslow, 2015.

Powell, William J. *Black Wings*. Los Angeles: Ivan Deach, Jr., 1934.

Rich, Doris L. *Queen Bess: Daredevil Aviator*. Washington, DC: Smithsonian Institution Press, 1993.

Riley, Ricky. "More Than Bessie Coleman: 7 Other Famous Black Female Pilots You Probably Don't Know." *Atlanta Black Star*, September 1, 2015. http://atlantablackstar.com/2015/09/01/more-than-bessie-coleman-7-other-famous-black-female-pilots-you-probably-dont-know

Tillinghast, Audrey. Tape-recorded interviews conducted April 21–22, 1991.

Zirulnik, Michael L. "Airlines' Flight Decks Lack Diversity." *Hill*, September 22, 2014. http://thehill.com/blogs/pundits-blog/transportation/218401-the-company-isnt-going-to-hire-black-pilots-anymore.

Index

Washington, Patrice Clarke,
107
Waxahachie, Texas, 9, 31–35,
31, 37–39, 42–43, 46, 49,
81, 91, 99
Wells, Ida B., 10
Wills, William D., 84–85
Wilson, Woodrow, 9, 25
World War I, 5, 13, 21, 23, 57,
64, 68, 70–71, 83, 110, 113
Wright brothers, 16–17, **17**, 46

yaw, 63

About the Author

Cathleen Small's interest in aviation started at the age of three, when her father would take her soaring above the skies of Wichita, Kansas, as he earned his single-engine and dual-engine private pilot licenses, as well as his instrument rating. These days, she spends more time behind a computer, writing books for Cavendish Square and other publishers, and editing for a number of clients. When she's not writing or editing, Cathleen enjoys traveling with her husband and two young sons—in the air whenever possible.